# AS-Level Sociology

## The Revision Guide

Exam Board: AQA

*Editors:*
Gemma Hallam, Kate Houghton, Katherine Reed

*Contributors:*

Charley Darbishire, Anna Hazeldine, Neil Renton, Frances Rippin,
Claire Thompson, Julie Wakeling, Andrew Walker

Proofreaders:

Sarah Acford-Palmer, Kate Manson, Kate Redmond, Edward Robinson, Jennifer Underwood

Published by Coordination Group Publications Ltd.

ISBN: 1 84146 963 7
Groovy website: www.cgpbooks.co.uk
Jolly bits of clipart from CorelDRAW
Printed by Elanders Hindson, Newcastle upon Tyne.

# Contents

## Section One — The Individual and Society



## Section Two — Families and Households



## Section Three — Health



## Section Four — The Mass Media



## Section Five — Education



## Section Six — Wealth, Poverty and Welfare



## Section Seven — Work and Leisure



## Section Eight — Sociological Research Methods



## Do Well in Your Exam



We deliberately haven't put answers in this book — because there are lots of valid ways to answer essay questions. Instead, we've put in a section about how to do well in your exam — which includes some sample 'A' grade exam answers.

# Culture and Identity: Theories

*This section goes through the basics of AS Sociology.* ***You won't be asked questions about this section in your exam — it's just useful background info which will help you understand the rest of the book.*** *Use this section to brush up on some of the key theories and issues — then move onto the sections for the topics you're studying.*

## Functionalism Says the Individual is the Product of Society

**Emile Durkheim (1858-1917)** was one of the founders of Sociology. In his view, society is made up of various **institutions**, each of which has a useful function. So, Durkheim and his followers are known as **Functionalists**. They looked at **how society was structured** — you can call Functionalism a **structural theory**. Functionalists looked at how institutions in society work, and how they **affect individuals**. Here are some examples:

1) **The Family** — has the function of socialising children.
2) **Education** — has the function of preparing young people for adult society.
3) **Religion** — has the function of uniting society through shared beliefs.

Socialisation is explained on pages 4-5.

Functionalists believe that the **structures** of society are set up to allow it to **run as smoothly as possible**. Durkheim was keen on the idea that individuals **internalise** the **norms** and **values** (the rules and ideas) of society. This means those norms and values **become a part of who you are** — your personality and your **identity**. The result is **consensus**, which means everyone sharing the **same norms and values**.

Durkheim called the **shared norms and values** that **hold society together** the "**collective consciousness of society**".

**Definitions**

**Structure** — the way **society operates as a whole**. Individuals have **almost no control** over this.
**Identity** — an individual's **mental picture** of **herself / himself**.
**Norms** — ways of **behaving** and / or **thinking** that are seen as **normal** in society.
**Values** — **beliefs** about what things are **important** and what things are **right** and **wrong**.
**Culture** — The **combined** effect of **norms** and **values** — a **way of life**.

## Not Everyone Agrees with Functionalist Thinking

1) **Interactionists** (see p.3) focus on the **individual** more than Functionalists do. They say Functionalism is **wrong to ignore the individual**. They think that individuals can choose how to behave, and aren't simply responding to social forces.
2) **Marxists** say Functionalism ignores the **unequal power** of some groups. Marxists say the rich have the most influence in defining the norms, values and beliefs in society. They think structures in society are set up to **serve the interests of the rich**, not to keep society ticking along as smoothly as possible.
3) **Postmodernists** (see p.47) say **Functionalism is outdated** because it's based on the idea that there's only one dominant or shared culture. Postmodernists argue that today there's a **complex and diverse range** of cultural norms and values.

## Marxism Says the Individual is the Product of Economic Forces

Karl Marx

**Karl Marx (1818-1883)** was another of the founders of Sociology. He focused on the **effects of capitalism**. He thought that the **economic system (infrastructure)** of a society determined the beliefs and values of that **society (the superstructure)**.

**Marxists** believe that the most important force in society is **class conflict**

1) In **capitalist societies**, workers are employed to produce goods which are sold by their employers at a **profit**.
2) Only a bit of this profit ends up in the workers' wages — most of it's **kept by the employer**.
3) Marx said that if workers were allowed to **notice the unfairness** of this, they'd revolt. So, to **avoid revolution**, the **capitalist system shapes the superstructure** to make sure that the workers accept their lot in life.
4) **Institutions** like the family, education and religion **lead individuals** into **accepting** the **inequalities of capitalism**.

In other words, Marxists think people are **socialised** into a **culture** based on their **social class**. They think people's **identity** depends on their **class position** in the capitalist system.

## Not Everyone Agrees with Marx either...

1) **Functionalists** say Marx put too much emphasis on the role of **economic structures** in shaping ideas and beliefs.
2) **Interactionists** say he placed too much emphasis on **class** and not enough on individuals.
3) **Postmodernists** say social class doesn't have such an important influence on individual identity any more. They say people are defined by the **choices** they make, not by whether they're a worker or a boss.

# Culture and Identity: Theories

## **Interactionists** Say **Individual Actions** are Most Important

Many sociologists say that culture is actually determined by the **behaviour and interaction of individuals**. Theories like this are called **action theories** because they emphasise the **action** of individuals, as opposed to **structural theories** like Functionalism and Marxism, which are all about the big structures of society.

**Interactionist** (also called **interpretivist**) theories start with the idea that all individuals **interpret** society around them — people **try to make sense** of society. Interactionists say that culture comes from **people's own ideas** of how people **interact** with each other.

Interactionists don't say structures aren't important, but they do suggest that each of us **responds** to social structures in our **own way**. We aren't just products of socialisation — we all have **free will** and make **choices**. An important thing here is that the **results of individual choice** can be **large scale social change**.

For example, **Jonathan Gershuny (1992)** made an interactionist analysis of gender roles in the home:

It's always good to know a few details of the studies.

1) Some **women decided** they wanted to **work outside the home**. That's the **individual choice** bit.
2) Male partners then took on **more childcare** and housework. It became **acceptable** for men to adopt roles in the family that had been considered **feminine**. That's the **large scale social change** bit.

## **Labelling Theory** Says We're Given **Labels** which **Affect** our **Behaviour**

The **classic example** of labelling theory is the **self-fulfilling prophecy** of **educational failure**. This is where a child is **labelled** as a bad student and then goes on to actually **become** a bad student.

Very **strong labels**, e.g. "**criminal**" or "**pervert**" can take on what's called **Master Status**, which means they replace an individual's other labels so they're seen as a criminal and nothing but a criminal.

It's important to remember that labelling theory is a kind of **interactionism** — it says that the **individual** can choose to accept or reject labels. In other words, being called a failure will only turn you into a failure if you choose to accept the label.

## What do you know... **Not Everyone Agrees** with the **Interactionists** either...

**Marxists** say interactionists don't pay enough attention to **conflict** or to the fact that some social groups are more **powerful** than others. **Functionalists** say they don't acknowledge the importance of the **socialisation process**.

To **sum up** — here's a nice table showing the **main ideas** of Functionalism, Marxism and Interactionism.

| Functionalism | Marxism | Interactionism |
|---|---|---|
| Dominant in 1940s and 1950s | Dominant in 1960s and 1970s | Influential in the 1970s |
| Culture is produced by social structure to create consensus. | Culture is produced by social structure to disguise class conflict. | Culture isn't produced by social structure. Culture is produced by individuals. |

## Practice Questions

Q1 What's the basic difference between structural and interactionist approaches?

Q2 Which theorist believed in consensus?

Q3 Which theorist believed in class conflict?

Q4 Explain what is meant by 'labelling theory'.

## *Students of the world unite — all you have to lose is your brains...*

*Social structure, social action, consensus and conflict are key sociological ideas. If you understand them, many other topics will make a lot more sense. Make sure you can jot down a few sentences about what Functionalists, Marxists and Interactionists think about the relationship between individuals and society. Then you'll know you've got the hang of it.*

# Socialisation and Social Roles

*Most sociologists believe you have to learn how to fit into society, e.g. learn how to behave and what to believe. This process is called socialisation. It begins in childhood and continues throughout life. As usual in Sociology, there are different views about how it all works...*

## *Socialisation is the Passing On of Culture*

1) **Culture** is a key term for this section. It means the **"way of life"** of a society — things like language, customs, knowledge, skills, roles, values and norms. Culture is **passed on** through **socialisation** from generation to generation.
2) **Norms** are **social rules** about **correct behaviour**. For example, by queuing in a shop or wearing formal clothes to a job interview, you're conforming to norms. **Laws** are often norms, but sometimes lawbreaking is the norm. Making illegal copies of CDs is a good example of this.
3) **Values** are more **generalised beliefs and goals**. Ideas like "freedom of speech", "respect for human life" or "equality" are all **values**.
4) **Culture, values and norms** are **not fixed**. They **vary** according to the time and place. For example, British culture is different from American culture, and today's culture is different from the culture of thirty years ago.

Sociologists say that through socialisation the **norms and values** of society are **internalised** — i.e. they become part of everyone's way of thinking.

There are two kinds of socialisation — **primary socialisation** and **secondary socialisation**.

## *There is Only One Agent of Primary Socialisation — The Family*

**Primary socialisation** comes first. In **early childhood**, individuals learn the **skills**, **knowledge**, **norms** and **values** of society. This all happens in three ways:

1) Children **internalise** norms and values by **imitating their parents / guardians**.
2) Children are **rewarded** for **socially acceptable behaviour**
3) Children are **punished** for **socially "deviant" behaviour**.

Children who are deprived of social contact during development often can't function as social adults. In 1970, an American girl known as "Genie" was discovered. She'd been locked up by her father for her first 13 years and never managed to recognise even basic social norms.

## *There are Many Agents of Secondary Socialisation*

**Secondary socialisation** comes after primary socialisation and **builds on it**. It's carried out by **various institutions**. The most important are **education**, **peer group**, **religion** and the **mass media**.

### Education

The education system aims to pass on **knowledge and skills** such as reading and numeracy. Learning these skills is a part of socialisation, but sociologists suggest that **education socialises individuals** in **other ways** as well:

1) **Functionalists**, like **Durkheim**, believe that school **promotes consensus** by **teaching norms and values**. They also say children learn to value belonging to a **larger group** through things like school uniform and assembly. All this is important for **fitting into society**.
2) **Marxists**, such as **Bowles and Gintis (1976)** believe education operates a **hidden curriculum** that socialises pupils into **ruling class cultures** and encourages them to **accept exploitation**. The curriculum is the **content** of education. Marxists reckon there are two sorts — the acknowledged curriculum (maths, English, geography etc.) and the hidden curriculum (doing as you're told and not questioning authority).

### Peer Groups

**Peer groups** are made up of people of **similar social status**. The peer group can **influence norms and values**. This can be towards **conformity** or **deviance**. **Youth subcultures** sometimes encourage **deviant** behaviour, like joyriding.

Conformity = doing what society likes
Deviance = doing what society doesn't like

### Religion

**Religion** often provides **social norms and values**. Most religions oppose murder, teach respect for elders and encourage hard work.

For more detail on these agents of socialisation, look at sections 4 (The Mass Media) and 5 (Education).

### Mass Media

The **mass media** are very **powerful** in shaping norms and values in the audience. According to some sociologists (e.g. **Althusser**) the media have now **replaced religion** in secondary socialisation. This view can be criticised as being rather one-sided.

# Socialisation and Social Roles

## *Individuals have Social Roles and Status*

Like it says on the previous page, **socialisation** is the process that turns individuals into members of a social culture. According to some sociological perspectives, an important result of socialisation is that each individual ends up with a number of **roles**. These are associated with different sorts of **status**. This is a bit tricky, so concentrate.

1) Your **status** is your **position** in a **hierarchy**. You can have low status or high status. It's the respect and recognition others give to your position. The Queen is a **person, being Queen** is a **status**.
2) Your **roles** are the **behaviours and actions** you take on **because of your status**. In sociological terms, a role is a set of norms that go with a status. The Queen has to meet the public and show an interest, she has to speak to the nation on TV on Christmas Day, she has to travel abroad and meet leaders of other countries. These are all **roles**.

**Status can be ascribed or achieved**

**Ascribed** status is fixed at **birth**. For example the Queen (this is the last time with that example, I promise) **inherited her status** from her father (who was King, not Queen, obviously) when he died.

Headteachers, on the other hand, have **achieved** status. This means they've **earned** it through **education** and **work**. This is a **very important difference** for sociological arguments about gender, class and ethnic identities. It'll reappear on future pages, so be sure you understand it now.

## *Social Behaviour is Regulated by Social Control*

1) Socialisation puts **limits** on people's behaviour. The functionalist Durkheim called this **constraint**. If it weren't for internalised norms and values, people would **do what they liked**. Internalised norms and values are like having a **little policeman inside your head**, stopping you from doing wrong and crazy things.
2) Functionalists say that socialisation creates a **consensus**, where everyone has the **same values and norms**.
3) It's important for people to **conform** to the norms and values of society. When people conform to the expectations, they're **rewarded**. When people **don't conform** to social expectations, they're **punished**. Sociologists call these punishments **sanctions**. Sociologists call behaviour which doesn't conform to society's expectations **deviant**. (Learn those words, they'll be useful...)

## *Society is Diverse*

OK, **Functionalists** say that there's a **consensus** of shared values and norms in society. It's true that many values and norms are shared across the whole of society, but there's actually a lot of **variation** in society. There are **many different cultures** in today's society — society is **multicultural**.

**Postmodernists** are big on the idea of **personal choice**. They say that in today's society people have a large amount of choice in their actions and behaviour — and in the values that they believe in.

## *Practice Questions*

Q1 When in a person's life does socialisation occur? (a) in early childhood (b) in adolescence or, (c) throughout life.

Q2 Give three ways in which primary socialisation occurs in the family.

Q3 Name four agents of secondary socialisation.

Q4 What is a role?

Q5 What is the difference between ascribed and achieved status?

## *Conform! Obey!...*

*Socialisation is really important throughout sociology. It affects the way people behave throughout their lives — whether they're at school, at work, at home or visiting the doctors. Try and remember words like "deviance", "conformity" and "internalised values" — they're good to use in the Exam cos they make you sound like you know what you're talking about.*

# Class Identities

*Societies are divided up into different social classes. Politicians may talk about Britain being a "classless society" but in reality you can see that people do tend to group together depending on how wealthy they are. Think about the place you live in. If it's a town or city, I bet there's a posh district where the richest people live — with detached houses and numerous garages...*

## **Societies** are **Stratified** — Divided into **Layers**

**Stratification** means the way societies are divided into **layers**. The **richest** and **most powerful** are at the **top**, the **poorest** and **most powerless** are at the **bottom**. In between are lots of **strata** (which means layers, like the layers in rock) organised in a **hierarchy**. **Social class** is the main stratification system in **modern, Western capitalist societies,** such as the **contemporary UK.**

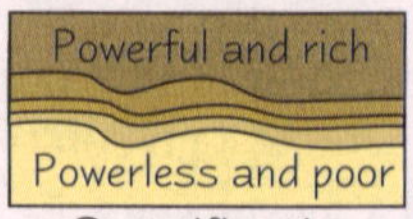

Stratification

## There are **Four Key Classes**

For the **Census** the **government** uses a scale called the **National Statistics Socio-Economic Classification** (NS-SEC). It has **eight classes** based on the **jobs** people do: higher management and professional, lower management and professional (e.g. teacher, nurse), intermediate (jobs without managerial responsibilities, mostly in service industries), small employers and self-employed (e.g. restaurant-owner, plumber), lower supervisory and technical (e.g. builder's foreman, sales floor supervisor), semi-routine (skilled services and manual work), routine (usually unskilled work), never worked / long term unemployed.

Sociologists usually talk about just **four basic social classes**:

1) The **Upper Class** are **wealthy** and **powerful**. The original upper class was the **landowning aristocracy**. Their wealth is **passed on from generation to generation**. People who have made a lot of money from business or from the entertainment industry are also sometimes considered to be upper class.
2) The **Middle Class** earn their money from **non-manual work**. Teachers, doctors, managers and pretty much anyone who **earns their living sitting in an office** are middle class. The middle class is **getting bigger** because there are **more non-manual jobs** these days, and fewer manual jobs.
3) The **Working Class** make their money from **manual work**. Farm labourers and factory workers are working class. The working class have **poorer life chances** than the middle class.
4) The **Underclass** get their money from **state benefits**. They include the long-term unemployed and the homeless. The underclass have **the poorest life chances**.

Sociologists have most often focused on the division between the **middle class** and the **working class**. Marx divided society into just two classes — the **proletariat** (the workers) and the **bourgeoisie** (the bosses).

## **Class Culture** Affects **Identity**

Sociologists often link **identity** to the **social class** of the individual. **Who you are** is connected to your **class culture** and **class identity**.

1) **Pierre Bourdieu** said the upper class **maintains its position** (on top, that is) by passing on **cultural capital**. This means the **knowledge** and **social skills** you need to fit in to the top strata of society. It includes things like knowing **which knife and fork to use**, the **"right" way to speak** and also an appreciation of **high culture** such as opera and ballet.
2) He also said that **middle class** families try to **develop cultural capital** in their own children in order to **improve** their class position. These parents **encourage** their children to read "good" books, experience theatres, go to art galleries and so on.
3) By contrast, he said that **working class** families **don't develop** this form of **cultural capital**.

**Barry Sugarman (1970)** argues that middle class and working class children are socialised into **different norms and values**. **Middle class** children are encouraged to plan for the future (**deferred gratification**) whereas **working class children** are encouraged to live for the moment (**immediate gratification**). Deferred gratification is a big part of studying and training for a **professional career**.

Sociological research, for example **Coates and Silburn (1970)** suggests that the children of the underclass are socialised into **feelings of hopelessness** which make them less able to rise through the social strata.

**John Scott (1980)** looked at the ways the **upper class** use the **public school system** (this means the **top private schools** like Eton and Rugby) to create **social networks** which then follow through into **high status universities**.

In the state education system, **middle class children** tend to form **pro-school subcultures** (such as homework clubs) and are more likely to be placed in top sets. **Working class children** are more likely to be **anti-school** and to find themselves in lower sets.

# Gender Identities

## *Sex is Not The Same as Gender*

In sociology, **sex** means the **biological differences** between men and women. **Gender** means **masculinity** and **femininity**, which are **not biological** but **cultural** and are **learned through socialisation**.

Sociologists focus on **gender**. One reason for this is that there are **gender inequalities** in education and employment that **can't be explained** by the **biological** differences between men and women.

## *The Family is the Primary Agent of Gender Socialisation*

**Ann Oakley's** research in the 1970s led her to identify **four** ways in which **family life** usually teaches children the **norms** and **values** associated with **masculinity** and **femininity**.

1) **Manipulation** — parents **often encourage** "normal" behaviour and interests for the child's gender and **discourage** what's seen as **deviant**. This **manipulates** the child's self-image — the child becomes interested in "normal" behaviours. For example, girls are often dressed up in pretty dresses so that being pretty becomes important to them. Girls are sometimes told off for being "unladylike" — shouting, playing loudly, getting mucky.
2) **Canalisation** — parents often **channel** their **children's interest** in particular directions. **Boys** may be given **construction toys** like Lego and **aggressive toys** like toy guns. **Girls** may be given **beauty toys** like toy jewellery and makeup, **mothering toys** like dolls and prams, or **housewife toys** like toy kitchens.
3) **Verbal appellation** — Parents may **use language and names** to **define what's appropriate**. For example, "you're an angel" (girl) versus "you're a cheeky monkey" (boy), or "what a beautiful little girl" versus "what a big strong boy".
4) **Different activities** — Parents may involve children in **different aspects** of the **household**. For example, girls help wash the clothes, boys help wash the car.

## *Education and the Mass Media are Important Secondary Agents*

Girls and boys are treated **differently** in **education**. Sociologists say that education passes on **gender stereotyped assumptions** about how males and females should behave. Remember that gender stereotyped assumptions can **disadvantage boys** as well as girls.

There are still **gender differences** in **subject choice**. Boys are more likely to study science subjects (especially physics) and I.T. at AS / A2 level. Girls tend to dominate in art and English literature.

The **Mass Media** help to build gender roles.

For example, **females** in Hollywood films are often presented as **weak,** in need of rescuing by a strong male hero.

**Angela McRobbie** (1978) has argued that teenage female magazines **reinforce conventional notions of femininity**, emphasising the importance of getting and keeping a man, being "beautiful" and so on.

**Joan Smith**, in her 1987 book *Different for Girls*, also argued that **culture creates** and **perpetuates** gender differences.

## *Practice Questions*

Q1 What are the four social classes usually discussed in Sociology?

Q2 What did Bourdieu mean by the term "cultural capital"?

Q3 What is the difference between sex and gender?

Q4 Name two secondary agents of gender socialisation.

## *I never liked pink much anyway...*

*OK, here you've got two separate pages on two separate topics. Cultural capital and deferred gratification are important concepts on the class page — sociologists are keen on figuring out what makes the working class different from the middle class. Gender socialisation is the key thing on this page — how girls are taught to be feminine and boys taught to be masculine.*

# Ethnic and National Identities

*British society includes many different ethnic groups. Ethnicity can be an important part of identity, as can nationality. Not to forget gender, religion, class, and occupation. One thing you can say for identity — it ain't simple...*

## ***Sociologists*** *Use the Term* ***Ethnicity****, not* ***Race***

Race is a way of classifying people by **visible biological features**, like skin colour or bone structure.
The idea of race is linked to **racism**, the idea that some races are inferior to others.

That's one reason most sociologists agree **ethnicity** is a better term to use when you're talking about society.
People from the same **ethnic group share** the **same culture** and **socialisation**.

## ***Ethnic Minorities*** *have* ***Different Cultural Features***

**Ethnic minorities** in the UK are mostly people whose families came here from former colonies like **Jamaica** and **India** in the **1950s and afterwards**. Statistics from the **2001 Census** say **7.9% of the population** are from ethnic minorities.

> Ethnic minorities have distinctive **cultural features** from their countries and **cultures** of origin. This means stuff like **values**, **customs**, **religion**, **diet**, **language** and **clothing**. These **cultural features** give each ethnic minority its **ethnic identity**.

It's a long time since the 1950s, so Britain's ethnic minorities have been through a lot of **changes**. The way **ethnic identity changes over time**, from one generation to the next, is something a lot of sociologists study (see below).

**Culture** based on **shared origin** is still an **important influence** on **ethnic identity** though. Some ethnic groups work hard to keep distinctive cultural features going. For example, **Ballard and Ballard (1977)** found that **Sikh immigrants** from the **Punjab** replicated many **institutions** of **Punjabi society**, and **encouraged** a strong sense of **ethnic identity**.

## ***Children*** *are* ***Socialised*** *into an* ***Ethnic Identity***

Quite a few studies have looked at the way **parents pass on ethnic identity** to their children.
This is primary socialisation — the socialisation that takes place as part of family life.

1) **Rosemary Hill (1987)** found **the family** was very **important** in the Leicester Asian community. She also said that some children learned "Western" ideas about marriage, education, work and so on from white peers. Hill thought this led to **generational conflict** between parents and children from ethnic minorities.
2) **Roger Ballard (1994)** disagreed. He found that young Asians **negotiated** the two aspects of their lives (home and outside the home). That meant that at **home** they'd behave in **traditional** ways to fit in with their parents, but **outside** the home they'd "**act Western**".
3) **Shaun Hides (1995)** studied the use of **artefacts** in ethnic minority homes. He was interested in the way things like **furniture**, **pictures**, **ornaments** and **religious items** helped **reinforce** ethnic identity. Hides found that the wearing of **traditional dress** was a really important part of this. **Women** wore traditional dress **more often** than men, and Hides concluded that **women** have the most **important role** in keeping ethnic identity going.

## ***Ethnic Identity*** *is Also Created by* ***Secondary Socialisation***

1) **Racism** in British society can affect secondary socialisation. For example, studies by **David Gillborn (1990)** and **Cecile Wright (1992)** suggest that Afro-Caribbean pupils are often **labelled** as a **problem** by teachers. This can lead to a **self-fulfilling prophecy** where pupils form an **anti-school subculture** because that's what the school seems to **expect** them to do.
2) The **peer group** is important too. Academic **Tony Sewell** said in an interview in 2000 that he thinks young Afro-Caribbean males are too influenced by popular culture. He believes that they encourage each other to be interested in **expensive consumer goods** (e.g. cars, the latest mobile phones, clothes) instead of **education**.

## *Some Sociologists Say that* ***Ethnic Identities*** *are a* ***Response to Racism***

1) When **Afro-Caribbean** and **Asian** families first arrived in Britain, they faced a lot of **prejudice** from the white population.
2) Some people from ethnic minorities felt there **wasn't any point** trying to **integrate** into the mainstream.
3) One way minorities responded to **discrimination** in work, housing and education was to **hold on** to their **ethnic identity** and **resist** fully participating in mainstream culture.
4) **Cashmore and Troyna (1990)** show how people in ethnic minorities turned to **each other** for **support**, for example in religious groups like the (mostly black) **Pentecostal Church**.

# Ethnic and National Identities

## *National Identity is about Feeling you Belong to a Country and its People*

**Durkheim** said that national identity (nationalism) has an important function. It makes **individuals** feel that they **belong** to a **larger group**. **Benedict Anderson (1983)** reckons that **nationalism has replaced religion** in giving people's lives meaning.

National identity can have **negative** effects. National identity can be used to **exclude** certain groups. If someone defines being British as being **white**, then they are **excluding black and Asian British people**. When an organisation excludes ethnic minorities like this, it's called **institutional racism**.

1) **Symbols** and **rituals** are important to national identity. The symbols of a nation's identity include things like its **currency**, its **flag**, and its **national anthem**.
2) Every nation has its own **national rituals**. These are events when people are **expected** to **think** about what it **means** to be English, or Scottish or French, and so on. A good example from Britain is **Remembrance Sunday** when there are processions and ceremonies to remember British soldiers who died fighting in wars.
3) **Sporting occasions** like the **World Cup** are another example of a national ritual – the **whole country** supports their national team, and the feeling of **belonging** to a country is **very strong** at these times.

## *National Identity is a Product of Socialisation*

**Schudson (1994)** says that individuals are **socialised** into a national culture and identity by agents of socialisation such as **education** and the **mass media**. For example, the National Curriculum says all children must learn about Shakespeare. The **hidden curriculum** also contributes by having school celebrations for national events such as the **Queen's Jubilee** or giving pupils time off to watch "important" national football matches.

The **media** are also very important in building up national identity. They do this by **broadcasting national rituals** – things like Royal funerals or the state opening of Parliament.

**Stuart Hall (1992)** writes about the way each country has its own collection of **stories** about itself. National identity is all about **learning** and **sharing** all these tales of **wars won**, **great sporting victories** and so on. These are **passed on** from one generation to the next.

## *It's Hard to Define a Particular National Culture and Identity*

It's **not really possible** to talk about one **British Identity** which is the **same** for everybody.

1) So many factors make up our national identity — it's hard to say which national symbols are important.
2) Another problem is **time**. Being British **now** is **different** from being British twenty years ago.
3) Then there are all the **different sorts of people**. Being 15 and British is different from being 40 and British.
4) Britain has strong **regional** and **ethnic** differences — Scotland, Wales and Northern Ireland have strong national identities of their own. London is different from Liverpool, and Asian British is different from Afro-Caribbean British.

A great phrase to remember and use in your exam answer is that "**there is no monolithic national culture**".

monolithic = universal, huge

## *Practice Questions*

Q1 What's the difference between 'race' and 'ethnicity'?

Q2 What makes ethnic minorities distinctive from the mainstream population?

Q3 Name three sociologists who have studied primary socialisation and ethnic identity.

Q4 What did Benedict Anderson say about nationalism?

Q5 Give one example of a national symbol and one example of a national ritual.

## *Beckham's free kick against Greece, England 5 Germany 1, etc. etc...*

*Sociology is full of these "hot button" topics. Debates about nationalism come up in the newspapers and on the radio fairly often. For you as a sociology student, the important thing is to know the main theories about how ethnic identity is learnt by socialisation — and if you know some key studies then that's all the better.*

# Contemporary Social Change

*Social class, gender, ethnicity and nationalism are all important influences on everyone's identity. These factors don't exist in isolation — they all combine together to make up each person's identity. As if that wasn't complicated enough, they're all changing over time.*

## *Many Sociologists say **Class Isn't** the **Most Important Influence** any more*

Most sociologists agree that identity used to be based on how and where people **earned their money** (social class). Many postmodernists say that these days identity is based on how and where people **spend** their money (consumption).

They also claim that people's **leisure activities** are **no longer class based**.

Traditional **working class** activities included things like **bingo**, **darts** and the **pub**. The **middle classes** were associated with **DIY**, **dinner parties**, **golf** and **bridge**.

Nowadays, lifestyles are based on **individual choice** rather than class background. Middle class people do traditional working class leisure activities and vice versa.

**Saunders (1990)** says this shows that today **individual identity isn't based on social class**.

To understand everything on these pages properly, and to answer questions on changes, you've GOT TO KNOW THE PAGES BEFORE — that's class and gender (pages 6-7), ethnicity and national identity (pages 8-9). There's also more about postmodernism on page 47.

## ***Gender Roles** Are Changing — for **Females**...*

1) In the **1970s**, when Sue Sharpe first researched **teenage girls' attitudes**, she found they valued **marriage** and **motherhood**. When she repeated the research in the **1990s**, she found that this generation of teenage girls stressed their **career ambitions**.
2) **Diana Gittins (1993)** looked at the **rising divorce rate** and said this was evidence that women's **attitudes to marriage** had changed a great deal. They were much **less willing** to **accept** relationships they weren't happy with. This was a sign that the old **passive female gender roles** were a **thing of the past**.
3) One important factor is the fact that more women **go out to work**, and earn good money. It is now more common for women to be the **biggest earners** or only earners in their household than it was in the past. The increase in office-based work is referred to as the **feminisation of the workforce**.
4) There has also been an **increase** in **female deviant behaviour** — for example girl gangs as studied by **Ann Campbell (1984)**.

## *...And for **Males***

1) Research by **Jonathan Gershuny (1992)** shows that **childcare** and **housework** are **shared** between men and women much more than in the past. The so-called **"new man"** does the dishes and changes the baby's nappies. Statistics show an increase in the number of **househusbands** — men who stay at home, cook, clean and care while their female partners go out to work.
2) One cause of men staying at home might be the **loss of traditional jobs** and **roles** for men. **Heavy industry has declined** and the majority of jobs now require **traditionally feminine skills** such as communication. Boys aren't socialised to have these skills as much as girls are, but girls are now socialised to be ambitious and dominant — traditionally masculine roles.
3) **Mairtan Mac an Ghaill (1994)** says these changes have led to a **crisis of masculinity** where **men no longer know** what their **role** should be. This idea says that men are **shut out** from their **traditional** roles, and are **not adequately socialised** to be able to **fit into new roles**.

## ***Masculinity** in the **Media** has Become **Feminised***

**Rutherford (1996)** points out that images of men in the media are now being used in traditionally female ways — i.e. to be ogled at. Male stripper groups like The Chippendales are a good example.

He also looks at the marketing of **men's cosmetics and toiletries**. There are far **more** of these products now than in the past, and the images used to advertise them are often of **half-naked male models**. These are signs that men's roles have moved closer to women's. Rutherford calls this the **feminisation of masculinity**.

Findings like this have led some sociologists to believe that **traditional ideas** of **masculinity** and **femininity** are now in **decline**. **Postmodernists** say that **both men and women** now see **consumption** and **leisure** as the **key factors** in shaping their **identity**, rather than masculinity and femininity.

# Contemporary Social Change

## *New Ethnic Identities are Emerging*

**Stuart Hall (1996)** talks about **new ethnicities** which are very **varied**. He says that the **old ideas** of condensing ethnicity to **white / black** are being **challenged**. There are lots of **different kinds** of Asian ethnicity and black ethnicity. Hall also points out that for ethnic minority people, **gender** identity, **class** identity and **sexuality** can actually be **as important** or **more important** than ethnic identity.

Many sociologists argue that **young people** from **ethnic minority** backgrounds are developing **hybrid identities** — based on a mixture of influences. **Paul Gilroy (1987)** examined how black and white culture has become mixed together. **Maria Gillespie (1995)** looked at how young Sikhs brought bits of **mainstream popular culture** together with **Punjabi traditions**.

**Tariq Modood (1997)** found that **ethnic identities** were **changing**. Things like wearing **ethnic clothes** were **less important** for young people than for their parents. **Younger** people were more likely to be **political** and **upfront** about their **ethnic identity**. On the other hand, **second generation immigrants** were **more likely** to **see themselves** as **British** or partly British than the first generation immigrants.

## *Traditional National Identity is on the Decline*

Some sociologists suggest that during the last 20 years, people have found it **harder** to **identify** with Britishness. British national identity isn't as strong as it was, and some would say it **doesn't exist** any more. There are a few reasons for this:

1) **Big business** is now **international**, and companies like the McDonalds burger chain appear all around the world. People in Britain are often **working for companies** based in **Japan**, **Germany** or the **USA**. Some **British companies** have been **bought by corporations** from **overseas**. Sociologists call this breaking down of national boundaries, **globalisation**.
2) Mainstream **TV**, **fashion**, **music** and **film** are often dominated by **American products**. Many people think that the result of this is that Britain and other countries are **losing their own cultures**.
3) Britain today is **multi-ethnic**. It contains many **different** groups, religions and languages.

## *New National Identities are Being Formed*

The old "Britishness" is partly being replaced by a **new multicultural national identity**. Things like food, fashion and music bring together **British traditions** with **multicultural influences** from **inside Britain** and **international influences** from the **rest of the world**. Our new "national dish", chicken tikka masala, is an example of this.

There are some **obstacles** to the creation of this new British identity, one of which is **racism**. A lot of the traditional British identity was based on the idea that the British were **different from** (and **better than**) the rest of the world. Some people may prefer this traditional view of "Britishness" and be **resistant** to the idea that British society and identity is changing.

**David Goldblatt** and **Montserrat Guibernau (1996)** are two academics who talk about globalisation and new nationalism.

## *Practice Questions*

Q1 What does Saunders say about identity and class?
Q2 When did Sue Sharpe carry out her research, and when did she repeat it?
Q3 What did Rutherford mean by "the feminisation of masculinity"?
Q4 What are hybrid identities?
Q5 Name one obstacle to a new multicultural British identity.

## *Class is dying, national identity is dying — but exams still live...*

*Seems like everything's changing. Which is a bit of a pain in the backside for you, because it means that as soon as you've learnt something about The Way Things Are, it all changes. But you can't expect society to stand still just because you've got an AS level exam coming up can you... No, really, seriously, you can't. That's just the way it is I'm afraid.*

# Nature and Role of Family in Society

*The family is one of the most important social groups for sociology because almost all people experience living in a family for some of their life. Studying the family provides evidence for understanding and explaining the links between individuals and society. First, though, you need to know what sociologists mean by "the family".*

## Families and Households are Not Necessarily the Same Thing

A **household** is a group of people who **live together** who may or may not have family or kinship ties.
The 2001 UK Census recorded **24.4 million households** in the UK. **Families** make up the **majority** of households, but there are other types, e.g. **students** or **friends** sharing a house or flat.
A recent **social trend** in Britain is the **increase** in the number of people **living alone**.

A **family** is a type of household where the people living together are **related**. Most commonly, a family is also a **kinship** group. Kinship means being related by **birth** or **blood** — parents, children, grandparents, cousins. Families also include non-kinship relationships — foster children, guardians, step parents and step children, mother-in-law etc.

There are two basic types of family:

1) **Nuclear family**: Two generations living together (mother and father and dependent children).
2) **Extended family**: Three or more generations of the same family living together or close by, with frequent contact between grandparents, grandchildren, aunts, cousins etc.

## Functionalists Emphasise the Positive Role of the Family

**Functionalists** see **every institution** in society as **essential** to the **smooth running** of society. A **key Functionalist study** by **Murdock (1949)** concluded that the family is **so useful** to society that it is **inevitable** and **universal** — in other words you **can't avoid** having family units in a society, and societies **everywhere** have family units.

> "No society has succeeded in finding an adequate substitute for the nuclear family…it is highly doubtful whether any society will succeed in such an attempt." Murdock (1949)

### Murdock (1949) looked at 250 societies in different cultures

Murdock argued that some form of the nuclear family existed in all of the 250 different societies he looked at.
He argued the family performed 4 basic functions – sexual, reproductive, economic and educational (social).

**Sexual** Provides a **stable sexual relationship** for **adults**, and **controls** the sexual relationships of its members.

**Reproductive** Provides new babies — **new members of society**.

**Economic** The family **pools resources** and **provides** for all its members, adults and children.

**Educational** The family **teaches children** the **norms** and **values** of society, which keeps the values of society going.

In the 1950s, American sociologist **Talcott Parsons** argued that the family always has **two basic and irreductible** (vital) **functions**. These are the **primary socialisation of children** and the **stabilisation of adult personalities**.

1) **Primary socialisation** is the process by which children **learn** and **accept** the **values** and **norms** of society. Parsons described families as "**factories**" where the next citizens are produced.

2) For adults, the family **stabilises personalities** through the **emotional** relationship between parents. The emotional relationship gives the **support** and **security** needed to cope in wider society. It's a **sanctuary** from the **stress** of everyday life.

Remember: Functionalists see the positive nature of the family as 2-way — it's equally useful and beneficial to individuals and society.

## Some Say Functionalists Ignore the Negative Aspects of Family Life

The Functionalist perspective has been **criticised** for **idealising** the family — focusing on the good bits and blanking out the bad bits. **Morgan (1975)** points out that Murdock makes no reference to **alternative households** to the family or to **disharmony** and **problems** in **family relationships**.

The **Functionalist** view of the family was **dominant** in sociology into the 1960s.
Since then there's been **widespread criticism** that neither Murdock nor Parsons look at issues of **conflict**, **class** and **violence** in relation to the family.

The fact that Functionalists **overlook negative aspects** of family life **makes their position look weaker**.

# Nature and Role of Family in Society

## *Marxists* See the *Family* as Meeting the *Needs* of the *Capitalist System*

Like functionalists, Marxists view the family as performing **essential functions** for modern industrial society. The key difference is that **Marxists** argue that the family **benefits** the minority **in power** (called the "**bourgeoisie**") and the economy, but **disadvantages** the **working class** majority (called the "**proletariat**").

1) **Engels (1884)** said the family had an **economic function** of keeping wealth within the **bourgeoisie** by passing it on to the next generation as **inheritance**. In other words, when a **rich person dies**, their **kids get their money** so money stays in the same section of the economy.
2) **Zaretsky (1976)** focused on how the family helped the capitalist economy. He argued that the family is one place in society where the **proletariat** can have **power** and **control**. When the **working man** gets home, he's **king of his own castle**. This relieves some of the **frustration** workers feel about their low status, which helps them to **accept** their **oppression** and **exploitation** as workers.
3) The role of women in the family in capitalist society as "**housewife**" means workers are **cared for** and **healthy**. This makes them **more productive** and boosts the economy — a great benefit that the capitalist class (the employers) get for **free**.
4) The **family household** is a unit with the **desire** to **buy** the **goods** produced by capitalist industry, e.g. washing machines, cars, fridges. The family is a **unit of consumption**. The family buys the goods for more than they cost to produce and the **bourgeoisie get the profit**.

All in all, Marxists argue the family is a **very useful tool of capitalism.**

## The *Marxist* View is *Criticised* for being too *Negative*

The Marxist view of the family is all about it being a **tool of capitalist oppression**, and **never mentions nice things**, like bedtime stories for the kids, or trips to the zoo.

**Criticisms of the Marxist view of the family**

1) Marxist sociology is entirely focused on **benefits to the economy**, and benefits to the working man's **boss**. It **ignores other benefits** to individuals and society.
2) Traditional Marxist sociology **assumes** that the worker is **male**, and that women are **housewives**.
3) There is **no Marxist explanation** for why the family flourishes as an institution in **non-capitalist** or **communist** societies and there is little Marxist research on **alternatives** to the family.

Functionalist and Marxists both see the family having a **key role** in society in **reproducing social structure and order**. The **key sociological debate** between them is whether this is **positive** or **negative** and **who benefits.**

## *Practice Questions*

Q1 What do sociologists define as a household?

Q2 What are the key functions of the family according to Parsons?

Q3 Explain the ways in which Functionalist and Marxist perspectives on the role of the family are similar.

Q4 Explain the ways in which Functionalist and Marxist perspectives on the role of the family are different.

**Exam Questions**

Q1 "The nuclear family is universal and inevitable." Discuss. (20 marks)

Q2 Examine the view that the family performs the vital function of maintaining the 'status quo' in society. (20 marks)

## Cog in society's machine or tool of capitalist oppression — you decide...

*If you're comparing Functionalist and Marxist perspectives about the role of the family, make sure you cover the pros and cons of each view — and most importantly make sure you answer the question. Remember, Functionalists believe that the family is there to keep society chugging along smoothly, and Marxists believe it's there to help exploit the common worker.*

# Nature and Role of Family in Society

*There's a lot of different feminist theory about the family — it's generally left wing and anti-traditional. But it's worth looking at recent right wing pro-traditional ideas as well. And at the postmodernists — who say everyone can do what they like. Hooray.*

## Most Feminists Believe the Family Exploits and Oppresses Women

1) From a **feminist perspective**, the **family** helps to **maintain the existing social order**. (If that sounds familiar, it's because Functionalists and Marxists also talk about keeping up the existing social order.)
2) Feminists call the existing social order **patriarchy**. Patriarchy is the **combination of systems, ideologies and cultural practices** which make sure that **men** have power.
3) Feminist theory argues that the family **supports** and reproduces **inequalities** between men and women.
4) The idea is that women are **oppressed** because they're **socialised** to be **dependent** on men — and to put themselves in second place to men. The **family** has a central role in this socialisation — **male and female roles** and **expectations** are **formed in the family** and then **carried on into wider society**.
5) Feminist sociologists say that there's an **ideology** about men's **roles** and women's **roles** in the family.

An ideology is a set of ideas about the way things are and the way things ought to be.

## There are Three Main Strands of Feminist Thought on the Family

The three strands of feminist thought are **Marxist feminism**, **radical feminism**, and **liberal feminism**.

The distinction between the three theories comes from what they see as the **root cause of patriarchy**. For radical feminists it's the **power dominance of men**, for Marxist feminists it's the **capitalist system** and for liberal feminists it's **cultural attitudes** and laws that allow **discrimination**.

All these theories generalise quite a bit.

### Marxist feminism — key points

**Marxist feminism** sees the **exploitation of women** as essential to the success of **capitalism**. The family produces and cares for the next generation of workers for society at almost **no cost** to the capitalist system. It's cost-free because society accepts that **housework** should be **unpaid**. Men are paid for work outside the home, but **women aren't paid** for work **inside** the home. If this sounds out-dated, remember evidence shows that even when women work outside the home they still do **most** of the domestic labour (see p.20-21). **Benston (1969)** points out that if housework were paid even at **minimum wage** levels it would **damage capitalist profits** hugely. **Ansley (1972)** thinks that men take out their frustration and stress from work on women, instead of challenging the capitalist system.

### Radical feminism — key points

**Radical feminist** theory also highlights **housework** as an area of **exploitation of women** but... and it's a big but... radical feminists don't see this as the fault of the capitalist system. Radical feminists see exploitation of women as being down to the **domination of men in society**. Radical feminism believes that **men will always oppress women**. **Delphy and Leonard (1992)** are radical feminists who see the family as a patriarchal institution in which **women do most of the work** and **men get most of the benefit**.

### Liberal feminism — key points

**Liberal feminists** emphasise the **cultural norms** and **values** which are reinforced by the family and by other institutions in society. The family is only sexist because it **supports mainstream culture** which is sexist. Liberal feminists believe **social change is possible**. They try to put pressure on institutions such as the **legal system** and **government** to change laws and social policies which discriminate against women.

## Feminist Theory has been Criticised

1) Feminist theory of all strands has been **criticised** for portraying women as **too passive**. It plays down the ability of individual women to **make changes** and **improve** their situation.
2) Feminist sociology **doesn't acknowledge** that **power might be shared** within a family.
3) Some feminist theory has been criticised for **not considering** the households in society which **don't** feature a **man and woman partnership**, e.g. **lesbian** and **gay** relationships and **single-parent** households. The power structures in those families **don't get looked at**.
4) Some **black feminists** have pointed out that a lot of feminist theory doesn't address the fact that women from different **ethnic backgrounds** have different **life experiences**.

# Nature and Role of Family in Society

## *The **New Right** Believe the **Nuclear Family** is the **Bedrock of Society***

1) **New Right theory** developed in sociology in the **1980s**. It's based on the idea that the **traditional nuclear family** and its **values** (mum, dad and kids, parents married, dad in paid employment) are best for society.
2) New Right theorists reckon that **social policies** on family, children, divorce and welfare have **undermined** the **family**.
3) **Charles Murray** is a New Right sociologist who says the traditional family is under threat. **Murray (1989)** says that **welfare benefits** are **too high** and create a "**culture of dependency**" where an individual finds it easy and acceptable to take benefits rather than work.
4) New Right theorists are particularly concerned about giving lots of **welfare benefits** to **single mothers**. They also think that it's a very **bad idea** to have children brought up in families where adults aren't working.
5) New Right sociologists believe that the increase in **lone-parent** and **reconstituted** (step) families and the easier access to **divorce** have led to a **breakdown in traditional values**. They say that this causes social problems such as **crime** to increase.
6) Some politicians have made use of the New Right theory. It's had an influence on **social policy** — making it **harder** for people to **get benefits**.

There's more about the New Right on page 64.

Pine cladding — that's the real bedrock of society

New Right theory has been **criticised** for "**blaming the victim**" for their problems.

## ***Postmodernists** Say **Diversity** in Family Structures is a **Good Thing***

1) The **central idea** of **postmodern views of the family** is that there's a much **wider range** of **living options** available these days — because of social and cultural changes. There are traditional nuclear families, stepfamilies, cohabiting unmarried couples, single people flatsharing, more divorced people etc.
2) Postmodern sociologist **Judith Stacey (1990)** reckons there's **such a diversity** of family types, relationships and lifestyles that there'll **never** be **one dominant type** of family in Western culture again. She says that "Western family arrangements are **diverse**, **fluid** and **unresolved**". This means a person can move from one family structure into another, and not get stuck with one fixed family structure.
3) Postmodernists say the **key thing** is the idea that contemporary living is so **flexible** that one individual can experience lots of different types of family in their lifetime. Postmodernists see this **diversity** and **flexibility** as **positive** — because it means individuals can always **choose** from several options depending on what suits their **personal needs** and lifestyle. People aren't hemmed in by tradition.
4) Sociological **criticism** of postmodern theory **questions** whether this "journey through many family types" is really all that typical. **O'Brien and Jones (1996)** concluded from their UK research that there was **less variety** in family types than Stacey reported, and that **most** individuals actually experienced **only one or two** different types of family in their lifetime.

## *Practice Questions*

Q1 Identify three different strands of feminist thought.

Q2 Give two factors that make up patriarchy.

Q3 What does Murray mean by a "culture of dependency"?

Q4 Why do postmodernists think there will never be one dominant type of family in Western culture again?

**Exam Question**

Q1 Examine the view that the family serves to reproduce the unequal position of women in society. (20 marks)

## *If this is too difficult to learn, blame your family. Or blame society...*

*Another couple of pages all about different views of the family. Feminist theory is complicated because there are different varieties of feminism. Which one you go for depends on exactly how unfair you think family life is on women, and exactly whose fault it is. Don't forget to learn the reasons why sociologists say each theory might be wrong, or flawed.*

# Changes in Family Structure

*The average family today doesn't have the same structure as the average family 500 years ago. Sociologists suggest various reasons for this, mostly to do with people moving to cities to work in factories.*

## ***Industrialisation*** *Changed* ***Family Structure***

1) There are **two basic types of family structure** you need to know: **extended** and **nuclear** (see p.12).
2) There are **two basic types of society** you need to know.

   **Pre-industrial society**: This means society before industrialisation. It is largely **agricultural** and work centres on home, **farm**, village and **market**.
   **Industrial society**: This means society during and after **industrialisation**. Work centres on **factories** and production of goods in **cities**.

> Industrialisation is the process by which production becomes more mechanical and based outside the home in factories. People travel outside the home to work and urban centres (cities) are formed (this is known as urbanisation). Industrialisation in the UK started in the 18th century.

3) What you really, really need to know is **how these two affect each other**.

   In **pre-industrial** society the **extended** family is most common. Families **live and work together** producing goods and crops to live from, taking the surplus to market. This is where the term **cottage industry** comes from.
   In **industrial** society the **nuclear family** becomes dominant. There is a huge increase in individuals leaving the home to work for a wage. The key social change is that industrialisation **separates home and work**.

Remember — **industrialisation is historical fact** but the **nature** of the **social change** it created is **sociological debate**.

## ***Functionalists*** *Say* ***Industrialisation*** *Changed the* ***Function*** *of the Family*

American sociologist **Talcott Parsons** studied the **impact of industrialisation** and **urbanisation** on **family structure** in American and British society. Parsons thought that the dominant family structure changed from extended to nuclear because it was **more useful** for industrial society — i.e. the **nuclear family** is the **best fit** for **industrial society**.

1) Lots of **functions** of the family in **pre-industrial** society are **taken over by the state** in **industrial** society — e.g. policing, health care, education.
2) The nuclear family can focus on its function of **socialisation**. The family socialises children into the roles, values and norms of industrialised society.
3) Parsons said the industrial nuclear family is "**isolated**" — meaning it has **few ties** with local **kinship** and economic systems. This means the family can up sticks and **move easily** — ideal for moving to where the work is.

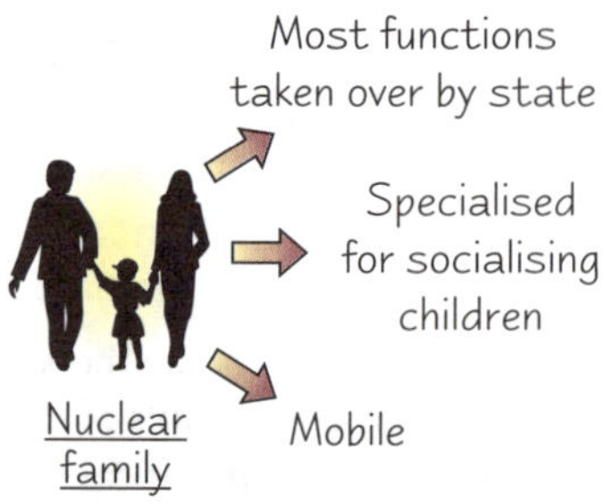


In short, **family structure adapts** to the **needs of society**.

## ***Functionalists*** *Say* ***Industrialisation*** *Changed* ***Roles*** *and* ***Status*** *in the Family*

Status for an individual in **pre-industrial society** was **ascribed** — decided at birth by the family they were born into. Parsons reckoned that in **industrial society** an individual's status is **achieved** by his / her success in society **outside their family**.

The idea here is that the **nuclear family** is the **best** for allowing individuals to **achieve status** and position without **conflict**. It's OK for an individual to achieve higher or lower status than previous generations. This allows for greater **social mobility** in society. People can **better themselves**.

Parsons says that **specialised roles** for men and women develop within the family. He thought that men are **instrumental** (practical / planning) leaders and women are **expressive** (emotional) leaders in a family. As a **Functionalist**, Parsons said these roles come about because they're **most effective** for society. **Feminists** and **conflict theorists** disagree — they say these roles come from **ideology** and **power**.

## ***Other Sociologists*** *say it's all* ***More Complicated***

Functionalists are **criticised** for seeing the modern nuclear family as **superior** — something that societies have to evolve into. They're also criticised for putting forward an **idealised** picture of history. **Historical evidence** suggests there's actually been a **variety** of family forms in the past and now.

Sociologist **Peter Laslett (1972)** reckons that the **nuclear family** was the **most common** structure in Britain even before industrialisation. His evidence comes from **parish records**. Also, **Laslett and Anderson (1971)** say that the **extended family** actually was **significant** in industrial society. Anderson used the **1851 census** for evidence. He said that when people moved to the cities for industrial jobs, they lived with relatives from their extended family.

# Changes in Family Structure

## *Willmott and Young Said Families Have Developed Through Three Stages*

British sociologists **Willmott and Young (1960, 1973)** did two important studies looking at family structures in British society in the 1950s to the 1970s. They mainly studied families in different parts of London and Essex. Their work was testing the theory that the nuclear family is the dominant form in modern industrial society.

You need to remember their conclusion, which was that **British families have developed through three stages**. (Initially, they set out four stages, but there wasn't a lot of evidence for the last stage, so they dropped it.)

| | |
|---|---|
| **Stage One: Pre-Industrial** | Family works together as **economic production unit**. Work and home are combined. |
| **Stage Two: Early Industrial** | Extended family is broken up as individuals (mostly men) leave home to work. Women at home have strong **extended kinship** networks. |
| **Stage Three: Privatised Nuclear** | Family based on **consumption**, not **production** — buying things, not making things. Nuclear family is focused on its **personal relationships and lifestyle**. Called "**The Symmetrical Family**" — husband and wife have joint roles. |
| **Stage Four: Asymmetrical** | Husband and wife roles become **asymmetrical** as men spent more leisure time **away from the home** — in the pub for example. this stage got dropped |

Husband and wife roles are called "conjugal roles" by sociologists

## *Other Sociologists have **Criticised** Willmott and Young*

1) Willmott and Young (and other Functionalists) have been criticised for **assuming** that family life has got **better and better** as structure adapts to modern society. They're described as "**march of progress**" theorists, which, I believe, is a bit of an insult in the world of sociology.

2) Wilmott and Young **ignore** the **negative** aspects of the modern nuclear family. Domestic violence, child abuse and lack of care for the elderly and vulnerable are all problems in society today.

3) **Feminist** research suggests **equal roles** in the "Symmetrical Family" don't really exist (see pages 20 and 21).

## *Different Classes Might Have Different Family Structures*

Willmott and Young's work in the **1960s** and **1970s** supported the **theory** that **working class** families had **closer extended kinship networks** than middle class families.

To get up to date, the **British Social Attitude Surveys** of **1986** and **1995** showed that **working class** families have **more frequent contact** and ties outside of their nuclear family.

Recent work by **Willmott (1988)** suggests that **extended family ties** are **still important** to the modern nuclear family but they're **held in reserve** for times of **crisis** rather than being part of everyday life. For example, if your house floods, you might go and stay with your sister, even if you don't usually spend loads of time with her. In Parsons' terminology this makes the modern family "**partially isolated nuclear**".

## *Practice Questions*

Q1 Give an example of social change caused by industrialisation.

Q2 What roles did Parsons believe men and women had within the nuclear family?

Q3 What is meant by the term "The Symmetrical Family"?

Q4 Outline one criticism of Willmott and Young's "march of progress" theory.

**Exam Questions**

Q1 Evaluate the assertion that the family structure in Britain has adapted to best fit the needs of modern industrial society. (20 marks)

Q2 "The British extended family ended with industrialisation." Discuss. (20 marks)

## *My mum works at Sellafield — we're a real nuclear family...*

*OK — here's something where it helps to have a vague idea about history, and about what this "industrialisation" business was. The idea is that when people went to live in cities and work in factories, society changed. Of course, it'd be far too much to expect sociologists to agree about it. Oh no. So you have another couple of pages of sociological debate...*

# Family Diversity — Changing Family Patterns

*These pages are about which family types are getting more common, and which are getting less common.*

## Social Trends Indicate More Variety of Families and Households

Official **Social Trends** statistics clearly show that the **variety** of family types has **increased** in Britain since the **mid 20th century**. There's now no such thing as "the British family" — there's several kinds of family structure out there.

**Look at the evidence:**

1) There were **24.4 million** households in the UK in 2002 — up by a third since 1971.
2) The **average size** of household is getting **smaller**. The number of households made up of **5 or more** people has **fallen** from **14%** in 1971 to **7%** in 2002.
3) You might think that more small households means more nuclear families. However, the percentage of households which are **nuclear families** has **fallen** from **33%** in 1971 to **25%** in 2002.
4) Two of the biggest **increases** have been in **single person** households and **lone parent family** households. This explains why the average size of households has got smaller.
5) There's been an increase in the **proportion** of families which are **reconstituted** families — also known as **step-families**. There are **more step-families** now that there's **more divorce**. In 2001-2, **8%** of all households were **reconstituted families.**

These stats are from "Social Trends (2003)"

The two **overall patterns** are:

1) There's been an **increase** in the **diversity** of families in the UK. There are more **different kinds** of family.
2) **Nuclear family** is still the most **common** type of family, even though the **proportion** of nuclear families is going down. In 2002, **78%** of children lived in nuclear families.

## Class, Ethnicity and Sexuality Affect Which Types Of Family You Experience

**Eversley and Bonnerjea (1982)** found **middle class** areas in the UK have a **higher** than average proportion of **nuclear families**. Inner-city **working class areas** are more likely to have a higher proportion of **lone-parent households**.

**Lesbian** and **gay** families have been hidden from the statistics. The **official definition** of a couple has only included **same-sex couples** since 1998.

The study of **ethnic minorities** by **Modood et al (1997)** found that:

1) Whites and Afro-Caribbeans were most likely to be **divorced**. Indians, Pakistanis, Bangladeshis and African Asians were most likely to be **married**.
2) Caribbean households were the most likely to be **single parent families**.
3) **South Asian** families are traditionally **extended** families, but there are more **nuclear family** households than in the past. **Extended kinship links** stay strong and often reach back to India, Pakistan or Bangladesh.
4) There's **diversity** within each ethnic group though.

## Fewer People Marry and More People Live Together Instead

In 2001 the **lowest** number of **marriages** took place in the UK since records began.

**This does NOT mean a decline in family life, though:**

1) Over the same period of time there's been an **increase** in the number of adults living with a partner (**cohabiting**). In 2001-2 a **quarter** of all non-married adults aged 16-59 were **cohabiting**.
2) **Social trends statistics** show that living with a partner doesn't mean you **won't** get married — it's often just a **delay** in tying the knot. A **third** of people who cohabited with a partner went on to **marry** them.
3) The **majority** of people in the UK do marry but the **proportion** who are **married at any one time** has **fallen**.

You need to know **why** these trends have developed.

1) **Men** tend to **die** before women. **Elderly widows** make up a lot of **single person households**. There are **more old people** these days, so this helps explain why there are so many single person households.
2) **New Right theorists** believe that the decline in marriage means a **decline** in **traditional family values**. However, evidence suggests cohabiting families actually have **similar norms** and **values** to married ones.
3) **Postmodern theorists** say the **role** of intimate relationships has changed — the emphasis is less on having kids and more on self-expression and emotional fulfilment. **Giddens (1992)** says that people are getting more likely to have a **series** of **cohabitations** rather than a **lifelong marriage** — this is known as **serial monogomy**.

# Family Diversity — Changing Family Patterns

## *The UK has one of the* ***Highest Divorce Rates*** *in Europe*

1) There's been a **steady rise** in the **divorce rate** in most **modern industrial societies**.
2) The **divorce rate** is defined as the **number of people per 1000 of the population** who are **divorced**. In 2000, Britain's divorce rate was **2.6** compared to the European average of **1.9**.
3) **Actual divorces** in the UK rose from **25,000** in **1961** to **146,000** in **1997**.
4) For every **two marriages** in Britain in **1991**, there was **one divorce** (source — Social Trends 1994).
5) The **proportion** of population who were **divorced** at any one time was **1%** in **1971** and **9%** in **2000**.
6) The average **length** of a marriage before it ends in divorce has remained **about the same** — **12 years** in **1963**, **11 years** in **2000** (source — Census 2001 report).
7) Although the divorce rate is increasing, divorced people are **marrying again**. In 2001, **40%** of all marriages were **re-marriages**.

You don't have to learn all of these statistics, but if you can learn some of them off by heart and quote them in your essays, you'll look very bright and shiny.

There are several **social**, **cultural** and **political** factors you **need to know about** when you're explaining why divorce is increasing in the UK.

1) Divorce has become **easier to obtain**.
2) Divorce is more **socially acceptable**.
3) Women may have **higher expectations** of marriage, and **better employment opportunities** may make them less financially dependent on their husbands.
4) Marriages are increasingly focused on **individual emotional fulfilment**.
5) The New Right believe that marriage is **less supported by the state** these days.

Availability and acceptability are the buzz words in the debate on divorce.

Remember — the **link** between divorce and marriage breakdown isn't completely straightforward. Some couples separate but never actually go through with the divorce procedure.

You **can't assume** marriage was **happier** in the past just because there were **fewer divorces**. A marriage can break down but the couple still **stays married** and living together. This is called an **empty-shell marriage**.

## *People are Having* ***Fewer Children*** *and Having them* ***Later In Life***

One very clear change in British family life is the **decrease** in the **average number of children** people have.

1) People are having **fewer children**. The average number of children per family was **2.4** in **1971** compared to **1.63** in **2001** (the lowest ever recorded).
2) Women are having children **later**. The average age of women at the birth of their first child was **24** in **1971** compared to **27** in **2001**.
3) More people are **not having children at all** — **9%** of women born in **1945** were childless at age **45** compared to **15%** of women born in **1955**.

Social changes have influenced these trends. **Contraception** is more readily available and **women's roles are changing**. The emphasis on the **individual in post-industrial society** is a key factor. Children are expensive and time consuming, and couples may choose to spend their time and money in other ways. The **conflict** between wanting a **successful working life** and being a **mum** has made many women **put off having kids until later**.

## *Practice Questions*

Q1 Which household types have increased in the UK in recent years?

Q2 What evidence is there that divorce has increased in the UK in recent times?

Q3 Explain the reasons for the trend of women having children at a later age.

**Exam Questions**

Q1 Identify and examine the overall patterns of family diversity in Britain since the 1960s. (20 marks)

Q2 "An increasing divorce rate does not necessarily indicate a decline in the popularity of family life." Discuss. (20 marks)

## *86% of people get bored of reading about divorce statistics...*

*Sometimes I wonder what sociologists would do without the Office of National Statistics, and their Social Trends reports. Anyway, jot down your own list of trends in the size of family, the number of single person households, the number of divorces and the number of people cohabiting. You have to know which are going up and which are going down.*

# Roles and Relationships within the Family

*As well as studying the place of the family unit in wider society, sociologists also research what happens within the family. The key focus is on the different roles and expectations of men, women and children within the family.*

## The **Rise** of the **Nuclear Family** led to **Joint Conjugal Roles**

**Conjugal roles** are the roles of **husband and wife** (or partner and partner) within the home. **Elizabeth Bott (1957)** studied how **jobs and roles within the family** were **allocated** to **men and women** in modern industrial Britain.

Sure, her study is **old**, but it's a **good foundation** for the debate so don't dismiss it — **learn it**.

### Bott (1957) identified two ways household jobs can be shared

| | |
|---|---|
| **Segregated roles** | Husbands and wives lead separate lives with clear and **distinct responsibilities** within the family. Man goes out to work and does DIY. Woman stays home, looks after kids and does all the emotional stuff. |
| **Joint roles** | Husband and wife roles are **more flexible** and shared with less defined tasks for each. Usually leisure time is shared. Responsibility for making decisions is also shared. |

**Willmott and Young (1973)** studied the changing structure of the British family from extended to nuclear (see p.16-17). They reckoned that the increase in the nuclear family meant that **joint conjugal roles** would develop. They predicted that **equal** and **shared responsibilities** would be the **future norm** in British families.

Willmott and Young's picture of **widespread equality** in marriage was **criticised** as soon as it was published.

**Oakley (1974)** pointed out that their study only required men to do a **few things round the house** to qualify as having joint roles. Their **methodology** overlooked the **amount of time** spent on housework — making 10 minutes washing up equivalent to an hour's hoovering, an hour's ironing and all the rest of the housework too. Oakley's research found it was **pretty rare** for men to do a lot of housework.

## **Conjugal Roles** are **Still Unequal** Although Most **Women** have **Paid Jobs**

Since the early studies by Bott and Willmott and Young, **new family structures** have developed. There are now lots **more families** where **both partners work outside the home**. Sociological evidence shows that an **equal share** of **paid employment** hasn't led to an **equal share** of **domestic labour**.

1) **Edgell (1980)** tested Willmott and Young's theory and found **none** of his sample families had **joint conjugal roles** in relation to housework. However, he did find **increased sharing of childcare** between men and women.
2) **Oakley (1974)** found that women took on a **double burden** — taking on **paid jobs** and still **keeping** the **traditional responsibilities** for **home** and **children**.
3) **Boulton (1983)** concluded that **men may help out** with specific bits of childcare like nappy-changing but **women** are still **primarily responsible** for children.
4) **Ferri and Smith (1996)** found that **two thirds** of **full-time working mothers** said they were responsible for **cooking** and **cleaning**. **Four fifths** of the same group said they were responsible for **laundry**.

These are all **small-scale studies** — it's important to look at research of a much **larger sample**. The **British Attitudes Survey 1991** was a **large scale study** of **1,000 married couples.** It showed a very **clear division of labour** — **women** did **most of the housework**. For example, washing and ironing was mainly done by women in 84% of households, shared equally in 12% and mainly done by men in 3%.

## **Industrialisation** led to the **Creation** of the **"Housewife"**

1) **Oakley** thinks that the role of the **housewife** was **socially constructed** (see p. 24) by the **social changes** of the **Industrial Revolution**, when people started **going to work in factories** instead of working at home.
2) **Married women** were often **not allowed** to work in factories. A new role of **housewife** was created for married women.
3) Middle class households had female **servants** to do domestic work. Working class women did it themselves.
4) The **cultural values** that said women should be in charge of housework were **so dominant** that domestic work came to be seen as "**naturally**" (biologically) the role of women.

# Roles and Relationships within the Family

## *Decision Making and Sharing of Resources can be Unequal*

As well as looking at the **division of labour** and tasks in the home, sociologists have researched how **power is shared** in the home. The traditional role of the **man** holding **power to make decisions** was **so widespread** that the phrase "**who wears the trousers**" is often used to mean who's in charge.

### Edgell (1980) interviewed middle class couples

He found that **men** had **decision making control** over things both husband and wife saw as important, whilst women had control over minor decisions. Half of husbands and two thirds of wives expressed a view that sexual **equality** was a **bad thing**.

Alas, no one knows who was wearing these trousers. It's a mystery.

### Pahl (1989, 1993) researched money management by 100 dual income couples

He concluded the most common form of financial management was "**husband controlled pooling**". He defined this as: money is shared but husband has the dominant role in how it's spent.

## *Explanations for Inequality are based on Theories About Power in Society*

Guess what? There are **Functionalist**, **Marxist** and **Feminist** theories on power in society.

1) For **Functionalists**, men and women still largely perform **different tasks** and **roles** within the family because it's the **most effective way** of keeping society **running smoothly**.

2) **Marxist** sociologists interpret the fact that men and women have different roles as evidence of the **power of capitalism** to **control** family life. They say women and men have unequal roles because **capitalism works best that way**. Even with more women working outside the home in equal hours to men, the capitalist class needs to **promote women** as "naturally" **caring** and **nurturing** to ensure workers are kept fit, healthy and happy. This role for women is maintained **ideologically** through the **media**, e.g. in adverts.

3) From a **feminist** perspective, inequality in household roles demonstrates **inequality in power** between men and women. A **patriarchal** society will produce **unequal conjugal relationships** because society's **systems** and **values** will **inevitably** benefit men at the expense of women.

So, all explanations of conjugal roles lead back to **different theories** about **power in society**.

These explanations all agree that different roles for men and women in the family help to **maintain the status quo** (keep things the way they are at the moment) in society — the disagreement between them is over **who benefits**.

## *Practice Questions*

Q1 Define the term "conjugal roles".

Q2 Describe the differences between joint and segregated conjugal roles.

Q3 What is meant by the "double-burden" of women in modern society?

Q4 According to Oakley, how was the role of "housewife" socially constructed?

Q5 Identify two areas of inequality in conjugal relationships other than household chores.

**Exam Questions**

Q1 Examine the evidence that conjugal roles are still unequal in modern British society. (20 marks)

Q2 "Power is the key to understanding relationships within the family". Explain and discuss. (20 marks)

## *I'll have a cup of tea while you're on your feet, love....*

*This is mainly about inequality in the family. You know, who does the housework, that sort of thing. Some sociologists look on the bright side and say that things are getting more equal. Others say they still aren't equal enough. Remember to look at the possible causes and social construction of inequality. And learn some of the statistics — it gets you more marks.*

# Roles and Relationships within the Family

*This page is about sociological perspectives on the dark side of family life — domestic violence and child abuse. Page 23 is about how our view of childhood has changed, and how social policy relating to childhood reflects this change.*

## ***Radical Feminists*** *See* ***Domestic Violence*** *as a Form of* ***Patriarchal Control***

First of all, here's some **evidence** of domestic violence in Britain.

**Dobash and Dobash (1992)** found that **25%** of all serious assaults recorded in the UK were on women by their husbands.

The fourth **United Nations Women's Conference in 1995** reported that **25%** of women worldwide experience domestic violence.

Easy stats to remember, those. Quarter of assaults in the UK, quarter of women in the world.

**Radical feminist theory** says **violence against women** is treated **differently** to **other violent crime**.

1) Dobash and Dobash's first UK study (1979) found the **police usually didn't record** violent crime by husbands against their wives.
2) Since 1979 the police have set up **specialist domestic violence units**, but still the **conviction rate is low** compared to other forms of assault.
3) **Before 1991**, British law said a husband was **entitled** to have **sex** with his wife **against her will**. In 1991 **the rape law changed** to say that a husband could be charged with raping his wife.
4) Evidence like that above is used by **radical feminists** to support their argument that **laws** and **social policies** in society have traditionally worked to **control women** and keep men's power in society going.

**Radical feminists** believe that **violence against women** within the **family** is a form of **power and control**.

"Violence was used by the men they lived with to silence them, to win arguments, to express dissatisfaction, to deter future behaviour and to express dominance." — Dobash and Dobash (1990)

The **social climate** helps to **maintain this situation** by making women feel **ashamed** and **stigmatised** if they talk about the violence. The shame and stigma are part of the **ideology of patriarchy** — the school of thought that says women should know their place.

Remember, not all feminists agree with the radical feminist view.

Shame also comes from the idea that women **should know better** — not get involved with violent men in the first place. There's a tendency to **blame the victim**.

Dobash and Dobash found that most women who left violent partners returned in the end. This was because of **fear of being stigmatised** — and because they were **financially dependent** on their partner.

**Abusive partners** often **condition** their victim into thinking that nobody cares and there's nowhere to go. The pressure not to leave an abusive partner comes from **the relationship** as well as from society.

## ***Radical Feminism*** *is* ***Criticised*** *for* ***Overemphasising*** *the* ***Power*** *of* ***Men***

There are **two main criticisms** of **radical feminist** theory of the family.

1) It **over-emphasises** the **place** of **domestic violence** in family life. **Functionalists** argue that most families operate **harmoniously** and **postmodern theory** argues that individuals have much more **choice** and **control** to avoid, leave or reshape their family relationships.
2) It presents men as **all-powerful** and women as **powerless** when in reality women often hold some power over men. The journalist **Melanie Phillips** (2003) highlights the fact that **women abuse men too** and **male victims** are often **ignored** by society and the police. The pressure group **Families Need Fathers** campaigns for men to have **equal rights** in **family** and child law.

## *Some Sociologists See* ***Child Abuse*** *in Terms of* ***Power***

Sociologists study the issue of child abuse by parents and carers in terms of power relationships. You need to be able to **explain abuse** as a **form of power** rather than explore **details** of abuse itself.

A parent or carer is able to abuse a child by **manipulating** the **responsibilities and trust** which go along with the role of parent or carer. Families are **private** and separate from the rest of society. This makes it less likely for children to report abuse.

**Social policies** have been **adapted** to give some **protection** to children. The **Children Act 1989** was set up so the state can **intervene** with families if social workers are **concerned** about children's safety.

# Roles and Relationships within the Family

## *Childhood is Partly a Social Construction*

Sociologists say **childhood** is not only a **biological stage of development** but a **social construct** (see p.24) as well. The idea that children are **different** from adults in their **values**, **behaviour** and **attitudes** isn't the same everywhere in the world, and it hasn't been the same for all time. In other words, it's **not universal** — different societies, with different cultures and values, can view childhood in different ways.

An example of this is how the school leaving age in Britain has moved from 12 to 16 in the last century. It would now be not only **socially unacceptable**, but also **illegal**, to leave school and work full-time at the age of 12. Effectively, the age at which childhood ends and adulthood begins has moved in line with social attitudes.

## *Aries says a Cult of Childhood Developed After Industrialisation*

Sociologist Philippe Aries' work on the construction of childhood is a classic study.

### Aries (1962) looked at paintings

Aries said that the concept of **childhood** in Western European society has only existed in the **last 300 years**. Before this, in medieval society a child took on the role of an adult as soon as it was physically able. Children in medieval paintings look like mini adults.

With **industrialisation** social attitudes began to value children as needing specialised care and nurturing. The importance of the child reinforced the importance of the role of the **housewife** — it was the housewife's job to look after children.

This '**cult of the child**' as Aries referred to it first developed in the middle classes and over time has become a part of working class values.

You need to be aware that although Aries' work is very important, he has been criticised. E.g. Pollack says that Aries' work looks weak because it uses paintings for its main evidence.

## *British Society in the 21st Century is More Child Focused than Ever*

There's now lots of **social policy** related to childhood. Children are recognised as having unique **human rights**. The **United Nations Convention on the Rights of the Child** was ratified (agreed to) in 1990 by all the UN members (except the USA and Somalia).

In Britain the Child Support Act 1991 established the **Child Support Agency**. This gave children the legal right to be **financially supported** by their parents, whether the parents are **living with the child or not**. This Act also made courts have to ask for the child's view in custody cases and take the child's view into consideration.

Children also hold more **power** in modern British society than at any other time in history. This has been identified by advertisers who recognise the **financial power** of children — this is often referred to as "**pester power**". Advertisers advertise a product to children because they know the children will **pester** their parents to buy the product.

## *Practice Questions*

Q1 What sociological evidence is there of violence between husbands and wives?

Q2 Explain the feminist argument that domestic violence is treated differently to other violence in society.

Q3 Dobash and Dobash found most wives who were victims of domestic violence returned to their husbands. What was their explanation for this?

Q4 Describe how the notion of childhood has been socially constructed.

Q5 List two social policies which have affected children in 21st century Britain.

**Exam Questions**

Q1 "Domestic violence is part of the ideology and practice of patriarchy in modern society". Discuss. (20 marks)

Q2 Evaluate sociological study of the child in society. (20 marks)

## *Brrrr... not pleasant, is it...*

*You'd be forgiven for thinking that the stuff on page 22 is all a bit depressing. Unsurprisingly, the main idea on page 23 is that childhood is socially constructed. Remember that it's not enough just to say that something is a "social construct" — you need to say how and why.*

# Definitions of Health

*Most people believe they're unwell if they don't feel like they normally do.*
*Sociologists see health as more complex than just not feeling poorly.*

## There are **Different Views** on the Meaning of **'Health'**

"Health" is defined in everyday language as an absence of physical symptoms of illness. This view is based on the **biomedical** model of health which is current in modern, Western societies. Some sociologists favour the **social model** of health, which sees health and illness as "**social constructs**" serving the interests of a powerful **medical elite**.

> A "**social construct**" is an **idea that's created by a society** — as opposed to an idea that's based on objective and testable **facts**. It's specific to the **values and behaviour** of that society — it's not universal. *But* people living in that society will usually **accept** it as **natural** and "**common sense**."
> For example, in **modern**, **Western society** it is widely accepted that **democracy** is the **best form of government**. This idea is a **social construct** based on Western society's culture, values and experience.

## **The Biomedical Model** says Health and Disease are **Biological Things**

The **biomedical model** is based around the idea that health and disease are **biological phenomena** which exist in an individual's body. **Disease** is something **physically wrong** with the body, and health is the **absence of disease**. The interaction of the individual and the social world is **not relevant** in the biomedical model.

Health professionals generally follow the **biomedical model of health**.

**Key characteristics of the biomedical model**

1) Health is seen as the **absence of biological abnormality**.
2) The human body is like a **machine** in that it needs to be **repaired** by treatment when it breaks down.
3) The health of society is dependent on the **state of medical knowledge**.

**Nikki Hart (1985)** identifies **five features** of the **biomedical model**:

| | |
|---|---|
| 1) Disease is **physical** | The **biomedical model** concentrates on **physical systems** of disease, not social and environmental factors. Disease happens in an **individual's body**, not as part of society. |
| 2) Doctors are an **elite** | The **medical elite** (doctors) are the only people sufficiently **qualified** and **skilled** to **identify** and **treat** illness. |
| 3) Medicine is **curative** | The body can be **repaired** with drugs and surgery. |
| 4) Illness is **temporary** | Illness can be cured by the medical elite. **Wellness** is the **normal** state of affairs. |
| 5) Treatment is **special** | Treatment of disease takes place in **recognised health care environments** (doctor's surgery, hospital), which are **distinct** from the environment where the patient got ill. |

Example: A **biomedical view of disability**.

The biomedical model **looks in** at the patient and tries to **fix** the disability through medical practice.

Medical practice is **interventionist** — it's something that's **done to** the patient.

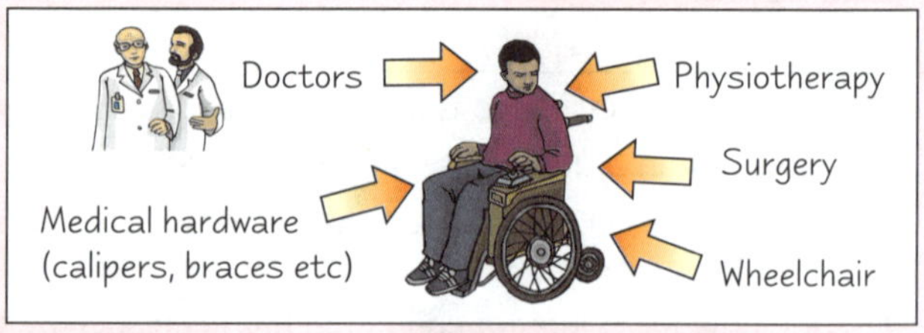


## The **Biomedical** Model has been **Criticised**

1) Some sociologists, e.g. **McKeown (1976)**, say that **improved nutrition and hygiene** have been more important in improving health — starting with 19th and 20th century public health reform.
2) **Ivan Illich (1975)** and others have argued that modern medicine actually **creates disease**. Medical accidents, infections in hospitals and complications following surgery are examples of this sort of thing. There's more about this on page 32.
3) **Marxist sociologists** in the 1970s accused biomedicine of distracting attention away from what they see as the real causes of illness — the **social causes**.

# Definitions of Health

## The Social Model says there's More to Disease than Physical Symptoms

1) **The medical elite** (doctors) **haven't always dominated** the definition and treatment of illness and disease — it's a modern phenomenon. For example, in the 1700s, mental illness was often thought to be caused by evil spirits — a religious thing, not a medical thing.
2) In modern society, illness is only recognised as illness if it has been **diagnosed** by the medical elite. The social model says **definitions of health and illness** are "social constructs" — not always related to real physical symptoms.
3) The social model says the medical elite have been **influenced** by powerful groups to **control** people's behaviour. For example, **homosexuality** could be defined as a "mental illness" by the medical elite in America right up until the 1980s.

## The Social Model of Health Emphasises Social and Environmental Factors

**McKeown (1976)** thought that the biomedical model was wrong in several ways.

1) McKeown said that **medical science** is **barking up the wrong tree** because it **assumes** the **body is a machine**. He thought this was a **mistaken assumption**.
2) Medical science says that **intervention by doctors** is needed to **protect** the body from disease. According to McKeown, **this is wrong as well** — external factors are the main reasons why people are well or sick.
3) Also, McKeown thought that the biomedical model **neglects** those "machines" which **can't be easily repaired**, e.g. the disabled or chronically ill. He reckoned that **most ill people** can't be easily put right again by doctors.
4) A social model of health would look to see which **environmental, social and behavioural factors** have contributed to make an individual person ill. There's more about McKeown's study on page 32.

Intervention means tinkering around with the body — by operating on it or giving it drugs, etc.

Example: A **social view of disability**.

The social model looks **outwards** from the individual to the **environmental** and **social** factors which disable an individual, e.g. lack of access, rights, and opportunities.

A person using a **wheelchair** might feel more disabled by the **lack of a wheelchair ramp** than the fact they can't use their legs to walk.

The social model of health **challenges** the idea that **wellness** is the normal state of affairs. Individuals with an illness are seen as **"living with"** their condition instead of having something **"wrong"** with them.

## Practice Questions

Q1 Why are doctors seen as part of a "medical elite"?

Q2 List the five main features of the biomedical model of health and illness.

Q3 What were McKeown's criticisms of the biomedical model?

**Exam Questions**

Q1 Identify and briefly explain two differences between the biomedical and the social view of health. (8 marks)

Q2 Examine how social and environmental factors might be said to contribute to disability and illness. (20 marks)

## All I care about is why do I feel ill...

*Hmm... the social model of illness seems a bit odd at first — how can it be society's fault that I've got a sore throat... But when you look into it, you have to admit that things like clean water, proper sewers and good diet are at least relevant to health. As always, you're expected to know the key points of each theory, as well as their faults and pitfalls.*

# Inequalities in Health

*The working class tend to suffer worse health than higher social groups. Some sociologists blame the workers themselves for their lifestyle choices, others blame the capitalist society.*

## **Studies** Show **Working Class** People have **Relatively Poor Health**

1) The **working class** have a **higher infant mortality rate** than the national average. The **wealthiest social groups** have **lower infant mortality rates** than the national average.
2) **Working class** people are statistically **more likely** to suffer from **serious medical conditions** such as heart disease, strokes and cancer.
3) **Working class** people are more likely to **die before retirement** age than the average.
4) According to government statistics, people born in **social class 1** (professional) can expect to live for **seven years longer** than people born in **social class 5** (manual workers).
5) People in the **south** of England are healthier and live longer than those in the **north**.
6) Some **ethnic minority groups** have a much higher infant mortality rate than the national average.
7) In general, **women live longer** than men.

These statistics are from the Social Trends report that the Office of National Statistics produces.

If getting ill was **pure chance**, you'd **expect** disease rates and life expectancy to be **the same across the board**. They **aren't**. So it **can't** be pure chance.

## **Cultural Deprivation Theory** blames **Bad Health** on **Working Class Values**

**Cultural deprivation theory** says that the **working class** lead **relatively unhealthy lifestyles** with relatively poor diets, more smoking, less exercise and more drinking. Their poor health is therefore blamed on their **values** and their **choices**.

1) **Cultural deprivationists** think that working class people are **less likely** to do **exercise**.
2) Cultural deprivation theory also says that the working class are less likely to take advantage of NHS **public health measures** such as **vaccinations**, **health screening** and **ante-natal care**.
3) **Howlett and Ashley (1991)** found that **middle class** people are better **informed** about health, with more **understanding** of health issues. Therefore, they tend to follow **healthier lifestyles**.

**Cultural deprivation theory** suggests that society needs better **health education** to make people more **aware** of health issues. It's resulted in lots of **government initiatives** through the **Health Education Authority** — trying to get people to give up smoking, eat less fatty food, etc.

## Cultural Deprivation Theory has been **Criticised**

Sociologists who **disagree** with **cultural deprivation theory** point out that **working class behaviour** is more **likely** to be caused by **real material deprivation**. They **don't think** it's an expression of different **cultural values**.

1) **Healthy diets** can be **expensive**, and **gyms** are often **very expensive**.
2) **Smoking and drinking** may be related to **stressful lives**, not **cultural values**.
3) Working class people are **less likely** to be able to afford **private health care**.
4) The fact that working class people often **don't take advantage** of **public health facilities** has also been blamed on feeling **intimidated** by health care and **health care professionals.** Health care professionals are **mostly middle class** and health care in general seems like it's set up to suit middle class people.

Work it, baybee, work it.

So it **might** not be the patient's own fault after all...
...and like so much in Sociology, it might be **a little bit of both** — a bit of smoking because you feel like it, a bit of not going to the gym because it's so expensive...

# Inequalities in Health

## *Social Administration Theory* Blames *Unequal Distribution* of *NHS Resources*

1) The **quality** of health care **isn't the same** across all areas of the UK. This is often called the "**postcode lottery**" — the quality of hospital or clinic you get to go to depends on where you live (your postcode in other words).
2) **Julian Tudor Hart (1971)** wrote "The availability of good medical care tends to **vary inversely** with the **need** for it in the population served". In other words, those with the **most** need for health care get **least**, and those with the **least** need get **most**. This is called the **Inverse Care Law**.

Another important report, the "Inequalities in Health Working Group Report (1981)" (also known as the Black Report), confirmed the Inverse Care Law.

Tudor Hart's conclusion can be seen as **out of date** — a tremendous amount of reform to the structure of the NHS has gone on between 1979 and 2004.

**Some sociologists** have criticised his conclusions by saying he **didn't have hard evidence**.

On the **other hand**, politicians still talk about the "postcode lottery" of the healthcare system.

## *Marxists* Blame the *Exploitative Nature* of the *Capitalist System*

now there's a surprise...

OK, remember that Marxists define **capitalism** as "**commodity production**" (a commodity is a product for sale in the marketplace, for profit). Marxists tend to see healthcare in capitalist societies as **just another commodity**.

According to **Doyal and Pennell (1979)**, the **pursuit of profit** has **negative health consequences** for the working class:

1) **Physical health consequences**

**Industrial accidents** and **industrial diseases** are far more common in the **working class**. **Keeping workers safe** from these risks would **cost money** and **eat into profits**.

2) **Economic consequences**

Capitalism **keeps wages low** to **keep profits high**. Marxists say this makes the working class **poor**, and poor people have higher health risks.

3) **Psychological health consequences**

**Workers** doing **repetitive tasks** on a production line are more likely to suffer from **stress related** health problems than workers with more varied roles.

**Critics** of the Marxist view point out that people in **communist countries often have poor health**, and that **Western capitalist society** has made a lot of **advances in health care**.

## *Marxists Disagree* about whether the *NHS* has *Reduced Inequality*

**Ian Gough (1979)** saw the NHS as a **good achievement** that the **working class** gained through political action. He pointed out that health provision for workers was pretty lousy before **1947**.

**Vicente Navarro (1976)** wasn't keen on the NHS. He thought that the NHS and biomedical elite played an **ideological** role — drawing attention **away** from the **social** and **environmental** causes of disease and illness (see p.24-25 for more on the medical elite, and the social model of illness).

Navarro also suggests that the NHS helps give the **illusion** that capitalist society is a **caring** society.

## *Practice Questions*

Q1 According to cultural deprivation theory, why do working class people have poorer health than middle class people?

Q2 What is meant by the Inverse Care Law?

Q3 Outline some criticisms of the Inverse Care Law.

**Exam Question**

Q1 Identify and explain inequalities in health and health care provision in relation to social class. (20 marks)

## *Everyone blames someone...*

*An awful lot of this sociology business is about blaming some system or another for the World's problems. Usual scapegoats are "working class values" and "the capitalist system". Marxists blame absolutely everything on the capitalist system. Make sure you know what the Inverse Care Law is — it's important for this whole module.*

# Access to Health Care

*The National Health Service was set up to give free and equal health care for all. It was mostly a success. Mostly.*

## There are **Inequalities** in the Health Care **Provided** by the **NHS**

The **NHS** was set up in 1947. It aimed to provide **free** and **equal** health care for **everyone** in the country. Unfortunately, although the NHS was **generally a success**, it **doesn't give 100% equal health care** to all.

1) NHS **money** is **shared out unequally** between different areas of the country.
2) NHS money is **spent differently** in different areas of the country.
3) **Specialist** hospitals, e.g. heart hospitals, **aren't spread out equally** across the country.
4) There's a **north-south divide** in the **supply of health care**, as well as in people's health.

See p. 27 for more on the "postcode lottery"

Sociologists and politicians often claim that there's a **two-tier system** in the NHS — which means that it provides a **lower level of care** to some, and a **higher level of care** to others.

**Politicians** have introduced **lots of reforms** to try to **make the NHS work better** and **make it cost less money**.

## The **Internal Market** in the NHS had **Good** and **Bad Consequences**

In the **1980s**, Mrs Thatcher's Conservative government tried to **reform** the NHS to make it **more efficient** and **less expensive** (a lot of taxpayers' money is spent on the NHS). They introduced an **internal market**.

This meant that **health care providers** would **compete** with each other to provide services, and **GPs** would be **responsible for their own budgets**. The idea is that **competition drives prices down**. It's an **economics** thing. More **hospital management** was brought in to manage and supervise these changes.

The government **encouraged private hospitals** and **private health insurance schemes**. This was to take some of the **pressure** off the NHS by getting people who could afford private care to go private.

Like most things in Sociology, there are pros and cons, and lots of different opinions.

**Positive Consequences**

1) There's **more choice** for some "health care consumers" (patients).
2) **Competition** tends to **drive down costs**.
3) In some cases, health care became **more responsive to local needs**.

**Negative consequences**

1) **Inner city GPs** look after **more people** and **sicker people** than GPs in **middle class** areas. **Money has to go further**, so inner city GPs can't afford the same quality of treatment — it's a **two tier system**.
2) Increased numbers of **NHS managers** and **accountants** could be a big **waste** of money.
3) **Competition** between health care providers means that **two hospitals very close together** might offer almost exactly the **same services**. This can also be seen as a **waste** of money.

## Some People Worry that **Foundation Hospitals** will **Increase Inequality**

1) In 2003, the **Labour government** planned to set up **foundation hospitals**. These would be free to **opt out** of **government guidelines**, **raise their own money**, and **set their own priorities** for how to **treat patients**.
2) The plans for foundation hospitals were **criticised**. Critics pointed out that only the **top hospitals** would be able to become foundation hospitals — they'd get **better funding** so they'd be able to attract **better staff**. They claimed this was a kind of **two tier system** — the **best hospitals** would be given more money to **get even better**.

New Labour's **Private Finance Initiative** will let private investors pay for building new hospitals. Some sociologists think it's the first step towards a **privatised NHS**.

## **Most Health Care** in the UK is Provided by **Women**

1) Around **75%** of all **NHS workers** are **women**.
2) However, only **25% of doctors** and **13% of consultants** are **women**.
3) **Over 90%** of **nurses** are **women**.
4) Studies have also discovered that the vast majority of **informal care** of **children** and **elderly relatives** is carried out by women.

**Radical feminists** think the NHS is a **patriarchal institution** — in other words, one where men dominate.

# Access to Health Care

## *The **Inverse Care Law** can be Applied **Today** to **Inequalities** in **Health***

Remember the Inverse Care Law from p. 27.

The **Inverse Care Law (Tudor Hart 1971)** states that people whose **need** for health care is **greatest** are actually **least likely** to get it.

### Julian Le Grand's survey (2003)

Le Grand's conclusion was that the **middle class** get far **more benefit** from the **NHS** than the working class. The benefit the middle classes got wasn't in proportion to their actual health needs.

Le Grand found that the middle class were 40% more likely to get a **heart bypass** operation than the working class. Also, the working class were 20% less likely to get a hip replacement despite being 30% more likely to need one.

Even with something as simple as **consultation times** in GPs surgeries, Le Grand found that professionals were likely to get on average two minutes more of a doctor's time than working class patients.

**Working class areas** tend to have the worst health facilities, the **fewest doctors** and the **fewest hospitals**. South Wales is an example.

This evidence supports the idea that the health care system is biased towards middle class people.

Research by **Cartwright and O'Brien (1976)** suggests that **middle class patients** tend to have a **better relationship** with their **doctor** than working class patients. Working class patients said they felt like the **doctor doesn't listen**.

## *The **Inverse Care Law** Could Also Apply to **Ethnic Minority Groups***

**Ethnic minority** health needs were identified as **relatively high** in a report published by the **Department of Health in 1992**. Remember, "**relatively high**" doesn't mean "shockingly sky-high" or "loads higher than the white population". It means anything from a **tiny bit more** to a **lot more** than the **average population**.

1) **Heart disease** is significantly higher in men and women of **Indian** origin.
2) **Afro-Caribbean** people have higher incidence of **stroke**, **HIV/AIDS infection** and **schizophrenia**.
3) **Suicide** rates are **relatively high** amongst **Asian** women.

Some sociologists think that **ethnic minorities** have **relatively poor health** because they're **less likely** to get the **full benefit** from NHS services. **Various possible reasons** have been suggested for this:

1) The **cultural values** of the NHS might be **different** from those of some ethnic minority groups. Some advisers say the NHS **needs to adapt** to **fit** the **cultural values** of ethnic groups.
2) Some people from ethnic minorities, especially the elderly, **might not speak enough English** to communicate well with health care staff.
3) There's some evidence that **discrimination** and **racism** affect access to healthcare. E.g. Research in the 1980s found that **Asian women** in family planning clinics experienced racism.
4) **Some ethnic minority groups** tend to see illness and disease as a part of life you can't do much about — and **don't bother** to go to the doctor.

## *Practice Questions*

Q1 List the advantages and disadvantages of an internal market in health care.

Q2 What are foundation hospitals?

Q3 Give three ways in which it can be said that the Inverse Care Law operates in today's NHS.

**Exam Question**

Q1 "The people who need health care the most are least likely to get it." Evaluate this view. (20 marks)

## *In the great drought of 1811 they introduced a two-tear system...*

*See, there's that Inverse Care Law again. There's still inequality in people's access to health care. Some think it's getting better, others think it's not. Sociologists are most concerned about a two-tier NHS, and about discrimination within the NHS. Governments keep trying to tweak NHS policy to make it work better, or to make it cost less, or both.*

# Mental Health

*These pages will help you revise different perspectives on mental health in the UK.*

## *Mental Illness in UK Society is Unequally Distributed*

Sociologists and psychiatrists can't agree whether mental disorders have **physical causes** or **social causes**.

**Sociologists** have tended to favour the view that there is a **social basis** for mental illness. Given the **social inequality** in who has good or bad mental health, maybe the sociologists have a point. For example:

1) **Afro-Caribbean individuals** in the UK are **more likely** to be **admitted to a psychiatric hospital** than other ethnic groups. They're more likely to be "**sectioned**" under the Mental Health Act — **admitted against their will**. Afro-Caribbean men are more likely to be diagnosed with **schizophrenia**.
2) Women are statistically more likely to be diagnosed with **depression** or **acute stress** than men. They're also much more likely to be on **drug treatments** for **mental illness** — antidepressants etc.
3) **Working class** men and women are statistically **more likely** to be diagnosed with mental illness than **middle class** people.
4) **Single women** have **better mental health** than **married women**.

There are **different perspectives** on these trends including **medical**, **feminist** and **interactionist** approaches.

## *The Medical Approach is to Treat Mental Health as a Biomedical Condition*

1) The medical approach to mental illness focuses on the **abnormal individual** rather than the **environment** that the individual lives in. It concentrates on the **physical symptoms** of mental illness. For example, a **medical approach to schizophrenia** would say it's caused by a **chemical imbalance in the brain**.
2) The medical approach is **cure orientated**. It emphasises the importance of treatments such as **drug treatments** for depression.
3) The medical approach suggests that treatment is best carried out in the **medical environment** (e.g. a hospital rather than the community) and should always be carried out by the **qualified elite** (doctors).

Compare this with the key features of the biomedical model of illness on page 24.

1) In the 1930s, mental disturbance was sometimes treated **surgically**. Doctors actually **severed** neural connections between certain parts of the **brain**. This is called a **lobotomy**. It often had unwanted side effects, such as adverse effects on the patient's **intellect**. Lobotomies aren't done any more, although more refined brain surgery is sometimes used in extremely severe cases.
2) In the 1940s, **electroconvulsive therapy (ECT)** was used to treat depression. It's still sometimes used to treat very severe depression. In ECT, an **electric current** is passed through the patient's **brain**, to create a **seizure** a bit like an epileptic fit.
3) **Drugs** are used to treat all sorts of mental illness. Some drugs have **severe side-effects**.
4) Mental illness is also treated by **psychotherapy**, where the patient **talks** to a **therapist** who tries to get them thinking in a more healthy way.

## *Feminists see Women's Mental Illness as a Result of Patriarchy*

**Joan Busfield (2001)** thinks that women might be diagnosed with more than their fair share of mental health problems because of **sexism** in the **male dominated medical elite**. She thinks that doctors **label** and **interpret** behaviour differently depending on whether it's a man or a woman doing it. For instance, an **angry**, **stressed**, **upset woman** might be labelled **mentally ill** but an **angry**, **stressed**, **upset man** might just be "**overworked**".

Psychologist **Paula Nicolson (1998)** thinks that **post natal depression** is more a **social thing** than a **physical thing**. She disagrees with the standard medical view that post natal depression is a **mental disorder**, and that it's **normal** to be a **happy new mum**. Nicolson argues that it's **natural** for women to get **depressed** after having a baby.

**Marxist feminists** think that women's mental illness is caused by their "**dual oppression**" as **housewife** and **worker**.
**Radical feminists** suggest mental illness in women is a consequence of **patriarchal society** in which women have **low social status** and the **stress** of **housework**, **child care** and **social isolation**.

# Mental Health

## The *Interactionist* *Approach* Sees Mental Health as a *Social Construct*

**Thomas Szasz (1971)** reckoned that **mental illness doesn't really exist**.

1) He thought that what we call "mental illness" is really just another "**social construct**" — a **label** society uses to **control non-conformist behaviours**. He said that people who behave in a way that the rest of society sees as **unacceptable** or **dangerous** are defined as "mentally ill".
2) People who are labelled as "mentally ill" can be admitted into psychiatric hospitals against their will. Szasz compared **forced treatment in mental hospitals** to the **persecution of witches** in the Middle Ages.
3) Szasz prefers a **system** where individuals are **free** to get psychotherapy **if they want to**. He says it's important that there's **no threat of force**, coercion or **loss of liberty**.

**R.D. Laing** was a psychiatrist who wrote in the late 1960s. He believed that "mental illness" is really a natural response to being in an unbearable situation. He also thought that mental illness needn't always be a negative thing. He had an idea that **mental breakdowns** could turn into **mental breakthroughs**.

1) **Erving Goffman (1961, 1970)** saw mental illness as a **stigma** caused by **negative labelling**.
2) Goffman was particularly **harsh** on the **role of mental institutions** in **reinforcing these labels**.
3) He thought that individuals in psychiatric institutions have to learn to **conform** to their label as "mentally ill". He said they **lose their old identities** in the process. Goffman calls this process a "**deviant career**".

### Goffman (1961) studied patients and staff in psychiatric institutions

Goffman described how patients respond to being labelled "mentally ill".

**Withdrawal** Patient doesn't communicate with other patients — doesn't believe he / she belongs with them.

**Rebellion** Patient refuses to cooperate with staff.

**Cooperation** Patient plays along with the staff idea of how a mental patient behaves. Patient starts to act crazy.

The staff respond to the patient's "crazy" behaviour by **punishing** the patient — they take away the patient's liberty and privacy and they don't let them make choices. This is called "**mortification of the self**". It ends up with the patient losing their personality.

The patient becomes **institutionalised**, which means they can't manage on their own outside the institution. After this, the staff can start from scratch, building up a "sane" conformist personality.

If a patient said "I don't belong here, I'm not mad" the staff would think "that's just what a mad person would say, you must be mad".

This is what happens to Jack Nicholson's character in the film *One Flew Over The Cuckoo's Nest.*

1) Many sociologists have criticised the **institutionalisation** of mentally ill people. **Care in the Community** was introduced in the 1980s as an **alternative**. Mentally ill people are looked after in the community, instead of in institutions.
2) Care in the Community allows patients to **stay at home** and **make their own choices**.
3) It's also a **cheap** policy — which makes it popular with governments.
4) On the other hand, it doesn't usually monitor the patient 24 hours a day. **Seriously mentally ill** patients can stop taking their medication and become **disruptive** or **violent** in the community. Patients can end up being **neglected**.

## *Practice Questions*

Q1 Which social groups are statistically most vulnerable to mental illness?

Q2 How would a "medical approach" define and treat disorders such as depression or schizophrenia?

Q3 According to Szasz, what is mental illness?

**Exam Question**

Q1 Assess the sociological explanations for inequalities in the distribution of mental health problems between different social groups. (20 marks)

## *If you say you're sane, it's proof you're not...*

*Mental illness is particularly interesting for some sociologists because it can be as much about social deviance as it is about mental health. In Stalinist Russia, you could get locked up as insane just for saying something the authorities didn't like. It's scary to think of. Learn about the medical treatments for mental health, the gender inequalities, and the negative labelling bit.*

# The Role of Medicine and Health Care Professionals

*There are sociologists who dispute the role of the medical elite in improving public health in modern times. Some even say doctors are the cause of much illness and disease. Blimey.*

## *Medical Intervention* Hasn't Done a Lot of Good — According to *McKeown*

1) **McKeown (1976)** claims that **medical intervention** by the biomedical elite **hasn't had much impact** on improvements in health over the last 200 years.
2) McKeown thinks that big health improvements have been mainly down to **social factors** — things like **sewage disposal**, supply of **clean water** and **improved diets.**
3) The **social changes** that McKeown says changed people's health all happened in the **19th century** — before the medical elite came to dominate health.
4) McKeown uses evidence like **life expectancy** and **infant mortality statistics**. He points out that life expectancy went up and infant mortality went down **before** biomedical techniques came in. For instance, mass immunisation for TB (a biomedical approach) only happened after the death rate for the disease had already gone down.

The bathroom — where social health really happens.

## *Illich* Says the *Medical Elite* Actually *Cause Bad Health*

1) **Illich (1975)** defines **health** as the **capacity** to cope with the **human reality** of **death**, **pain**, and **sickness**. This is a very different definition to the mainstream biomedical definition.
2) Illich believes that medicine has **gone too far**, and started to "**play God**" — trying to **wipe out** death, pain, and sickness. OK so far... he then says that **trying to control death and illness** is a bad move which **turns people into consumers** or even objects. In his opinion, this messes up people's natural capacity for health and **makes people ill**.
3) Illich uses the word **iatrogenesis** to mean this kind of illness that's caused by modern medicine. He says there are **three types of iatrogenesis**:

> 1) **Clinical iatrogenesis** — the **harm** done to patients by **ineffective** treatments, **unsafe** treatments or getting the **wrong diagnosis**.
> 2) **Social iatrogenesis** — the idea that **doctors** have **taken over control** of people's lives, and individuals can't make decisions about their problems. More and more of people's problems are seen as **suitable** for **medical intervention**. This is called the **medicalisation of social life**.
> 3) **Cultural iatrogenesis** — **traditional ways** of **dealing** with and making sense of **death**, **pain**, and **sickness** are becoming obsolete because medical professionals now deal with nearly all our health problems.

**Illich** thinks the **worst** is **cultural iatrogenesis**. He puts it like this:

> "A society's image of death reveals the level of independence of its people, their personal relatedness, self reliance, and aliveness."

According to Illich's view, dying has become the ultimate form of **consumer resistance** (when you're dead, you can't buy any more Nike trainers, I'd imagine). **Death** isn't seen as something normal. It's become a **taboo**.

## *Functionalists* See Illness as *Deviant* — Doctors *Control* this Deviance

1) According to **functionalists** like **Talcott Parsons (1951)**, doctors have an **important function in society** — they control the amount of time people take off **work** and **family duties**.
2) Illness is "**deviant behaviour**" which **disrupts** work and home life — you're not supposed to take time off sick.
3) Parsons said that sick people take on a "**sick role**". While a person is sick, they're allowed to stop functioning in their **normal role**. They don't have responsibility for making themselves better — but they are **expected** to **want to get better**, and to do whatever the doctor tells them.
4) Doctors are in charge of **confirming** that the patient is **actually ill**. Doctors **allow** the sick person to take limited time off, and **make them better** by using their **expert medical knowledge**. Parsons thought that doctors always put the patient's needs before their own needs.

**Critics** of Parsons say the medical profession don't always put patients first — they say private medicine is proof that doctors are self-interested. However, it **can't be denied** that doctors really do give people **sick notes** so they can take sick leave.

# The Role of Medicine and Health Care Professionals

## Marxists see Medicine as an Institution Which Supports Capitalism

Marxists believe that the medical profession only do good for the **capitalist** class — they **keep class inequalities going**. Marxists say that the medical profession have a **conservative** role in society.

1) Doctors keep the workforce **healthy** and **productive**. **Healthy** workers can **work harder** and won't have to take **time off sick**. This means **more profits** for the capitalist class.
2) Doctors **check** that **workers** aren't spending **too much time on sick leave**. They say **how long** a worker can **stay off work**.
3) Marxists believe that doctors **hide the real social causes of illness** (poverty, class inequality etc.) by focusing on the individual and their physical symptoms.

Some Marxists think that **doctors** are **agents** of **large drugs corporations** — they believe that health care exists mainly to produce **profits** for drugs companies.

## Weberians see the Medical Profession as Self-Serving

Weberians think that doctors **arrange** things so that they **keep** their **high status** in society.

A Weberian is a follower of German sociologist, historian and economist Max Weber (1864-1920).

They suggest that the medical profession is **self-serving**.

They argue that the medical profession has managed to **shut out** other forms of healing such as homeopathy, aromatherapy, faith healing and other types of **alternative medicine**. This makes modern medicine a monopoly.

## Feminists see the Medical Profession as Serving Patriarchal Interests

1) Some feminists say that most **contraceptive methods** (e.g. the pill and IUDs) are designed for men rather than women. This doesn't mean men are supposed to use them — it means they have **significant health risks** for women that **men would never put up with**.
2) **Oakley (1984)** has said that the process of childbirth has been "**medicalised**". In other words, women giving birth are treated like there's **something wrong with them**. **Control** over giving birth is taken away from women and given to **men**. Male doctors are often in charge, not midwives or the women who are actually giving birth.
3) Women tend to have **subordinate** roles in medicine — **nurses** and **auxiliaries** tend to be **women**, **consultants** tend to be **men**. Some feminists think that the role of being a nurse has been made to look like being a "doctor's handmaid" — a female servant obeying the male doctor.
4) **Cosmetic surgery** is criticised by some feminists as the "medicalisation of beauty", and also as a **social control** over women.
5) Feminists see the diagnosis and treatment of **depression** in women as another kind of **social control**. There's more on mental health and feminism on page 30.

Of course, not everyone agrees that drugs for depression are prescribed to make women shut up and stop whingeing. It depends on your ideological viewpoint...

## Practice Questions

Q1 What does McKeown claim is responsible for improvements in health in the last two hundred years?

Q2 What three types of iatrogenesis does Illich identify?

Q3 What role do Marxists believe the medical profession plays?

**Exam Questions**

Q1 "Health and sickness are defined by the powerful". Discuss this view. (20 marks)

Q2 To what extent can the NHS be described as a patriarchical institution? (20 marks)

## If doctors make you ill, do teachers make you thick...

*Blimey, this iatrogenesis idea is a bit radical — it's actually the doctors' fault that we're ill... Still, you can kind of see some reasoning behind it. Oh, and as ever, you need to be able to compare and contrast functionalist (all for the best), Marxist (all set up for the benefit of the bosses), Weberian (all for the benefit of doctors) and feminist (all unfair to women) views. It's a right laugh.*

# Ownership and Control of Mass Media

*The mass media is one of the most powerful influences in modern society because it's part of all our lives. The power and influence of the media is so wide-ranging that it's important to know just who owns and controls the media. The media is also an important input into the economy, and makes some people very rich.*

## The Media is Owned by a Few Powerful Companies and Individuals

The **same companies** often own **different forms of media** — films, TV, radio and newspapers. This is called **cross-media ownership**. It's often not publicised.

1) Media companies **diversify** — they buy other companies that make **different kinds of media**, and companies in **other business sectors**. For example, **Granada** was the first UK media company to buy a stake in a **football team** (Liverpool). **BSkyB** own 9.9% of Leeds United, Chelsea and Sunderland and **NTL** own 9.9% of Newcastle United and Aston Villa. BSkyB tried and failed to buy Manchester United PLC for over £600m in 1998.
2) In the US, in 2000 **Time Warner merged with AOL** to create a **huge company** with massive power and influence. Time Warner was already huge (it owns CNN, New Line Cinema, and lots of magazines and record labels) and AOL is the World's biggest ISP (Internet Service Provider).
3) Some media companies **own media** in **several different countries**. Rupert Murdoch's **News Corporation** owns **Fox TV** in the **US**, **Star TV** in **Asia**, **BSkyB** in the **UK**, **Fox Sports** in **Australia**, an **international** TV guide publisher, the **New York Post** newspaper in the US, several **Australian newspapers** and several **British newspapers**. Blimey.
4) **Bagdikian (1997)** found only **ten** major companies owned **25 000** media outlets in America. Wow.

| Media group | % share of audience |
|---|---|
| BBC | 19.7 |
| News Corporation | 10.6 |
| ITV Network | 9.4 |
| Daily Mail Trust | 7.8 |
| Mirror Group Newspapers | 7.6 |
| United Newspapers | 5.7 |
| Carlton Communications | 3.1 |
| Channel 4 | 2.9 |
| Other | 33.2 |

This table shows "media concentration" measured by the time that British audiences spent using media owned by each media group. Source — Congdon et al. (1995)

The individuals who own and control those companies have **huge power and influence** in society. They can **control** the information we receive if they want to. A great example is **Italy**, where the **Prime Minister** Silvio Berlusconi **owns most of the media outlets**. Some people claim he is able to use them to **control the reporting** of his political party and the opposition.

## Marxists say Media Ownership Controls Media Content

Different types of Marxists have different views about **how** the media is controlled:

**1) Traditional Marxism — media owners control what we see in the media**

The idea is that the owners of the media **exploit their power position** to **manipulate** the content of the media. Capitalist media owners **tell news editors** what **stories** to cover and what **views** to put across. There's a lot of **anecdotal** evidence about newspaper proprietors **personally telling** the **editors** of their newspapers **what view to take on important stories**. The media ends up putting across views that **serve the interests of capitalism**.

**2) Neo-Marxism — what we see in the media reflects the ideas of the ruling class, including owners**

**Neo-Marxist theory** is **more complicated**. It says that control over the media is **indirect**. It's a bit vague and hand-wavy, but bear with me for two ticks... Neo-Marxism says the **world view of the elite class** is **broadcast** and **reinforced** by the media. The **values** and **ideas** of the **ruling class** (including media owners) are presented as the **only views to have**, or the **natural**, **common-sense** views to have.

## Pluralism says the Media Reflects the Values and Beliefs of Society

The pluralist view is that **society gets the media it wants** — media outlets have to **respond to market demand** or they'll go out of business. Pluralist theory says the media **reflects attitudes already present** in society, and **doesn't** try to **influence** society.
In other words, it **doesn't really matter** who **owns** the media — it's the **market** that matters.

There's a definition of pluralism on page 37.

# Ownership and Control of Mass Media

## *There Are **More Forms** of **Communication** and **Entertainment** These Days*

Since the sociologists began studying the mass media there's been a wild and crazy explosion in new methods of communication. The two biggest developments have been the **internet** and **satellite broadcasting technology**.

1) The **Internet** has made a phenomenal, **humungous amount of information** available to a massive audience.
2) **Email** and **text messaging** have become very popular in a very short period of time.
Text messaging at 10p a pop is a **big income source** for mobile phone networks.
3) New, **"third-generation" mobile phones** can carry a large amount of information — pictures, Internet, streaming video of news and sport, advertising etc. There's been a lot of **investment** in these — the **government** made an absolute packet **selling the licences** to run the networks.
4) **Digital technology** means you can fit a **whole lot more TV channels** into the airwaves. There are more channels broadcasting to more "**niche**" special interest markets — e.g. DIY, motor sport, shopping.
5) The growth of **digital satellite** broadcasting has meant a big change in the way that **sport** is funded — particularly football. Satellite and digital broadcasters pay big money to buy the rights to **Premiership games**, and terrestrial TV is left with a highlights package.
6) **DVDs** can include documentaries, screen savers, interactive features etc.
A DVD of a film has **added value** compared to a video cassette of a film.

There's more choice of media for the individual but not really much more choice in who **owns** and **controls** the media. The **large companies** have **expanded** into the new areas, e.g. Virgin now have an Internet Service Provider.

> In the UK, television is **regulated by the state** to make sure it **acts in the public interest**. Some say that the huge growth in the **number of TV channels** means that the public will soon be able to get **whatever they want** from TV. This would mean there'd be **no need** for state regulation. Not everyone agrees though.
>
> The fact that there are lots of channels **broadcasting to the UK from abroad** means it's **impossible** for the state to regulate the content of those channels.

## ***Merchandising** is Linked to **Media Ownership***

A **film** or **book** release will be "**tied-in**" with other products, e.g. each **Disney** film release coincides with a new range of **toys** and **gifts** with children's meals at fast food chains, films with **cult appeal** often have tie-in posters and screenplays sold through high street music stores (e.g. 'Pulp Fiction'). This merchandising helps **advertise** the film or book and also makes **profits** for the companies making the tie-ins, which are sometimes owned by the same **parent company**.

The **media** have also used technological advances like text messaging and interactive TV to make more money. Reality TV is a great example of this — think Big Brother, Pop Idol and any kind of show where the audience has a **vote** on how the programme develops. The **production company** behind the show **makes money** on every text vote, interactive TV vote or phone vote received.

## *Practice Questions*

Q1 What is cross-media ownership?
Q2 Explain how the ownership of the media in the UK is concentrated.
Q3 List three examples of mass media developed with modern technology.
Q4 Give an example of tie-in merchandising.

**Exam Questions**

Q1 Examine the view that the media is used as a tool to support capitalist interests. (20 marks)

Q2 "The content of the mass media reflects society". Discuss. (20 marks)

## *I own my own TV — I've got the receipt for it and everything...*

*The debate over ownership of the mass media boils down to whether media owners use the media to manipulate society or whether they use it to present all facts and opinions. I've got to say — if I owned a newspaper I'd be awfully tempted to use it to spread my own views. Just casually like, nothing blatant. You know, I really must stop modelling myself on Dr Evil.*

# Theories about Mass Media

*These two pages focus on ideology and theory and mention things like "neo-Marxism" and "pluralism" — which also appeared briefly on page 34. Page 34 concentrated on media ownership. These pages concentrate on the ways in which **ideology influences the media** and its content.*

## *Traditional Marxists Say Media Serves the Economic Power of the Ruling Class*

1) According to **traditional Marxism**, the media presents what's **important** and **relevant** to the **ruling class**. For example, stocks and share prices are featured on national news bulletins but only a small percentage of the population have a lot of shares. Marxists say that the poor are ignored by the media because they don't have money to buy the things that capitalism sells.
2) Marxist theory says that it's the "**logic of capitalism**" that the institutions in society will always be used as instruments of power by the capitalist class. It's all about serving the interests of capitalism.
3) For example, advertising is in magazines and on TV to **create the demand for goods** produced in the **capitalist economy**. Advertising also gives the idea that there's a wide range of choice for the consumer when, in reality, a few companies own the vast majority of products.
4) **Herbert Marcuse (1964)** was a Marxist who reckoned that the media promotes **consumerism** and gives people "false needs" — the belief that they "need" things that they don't really need.

There's more about Marcuse and his "false needs" on page 72.

Marxist sociologist **Miliband (1969)** thought that the media encourages the proletariat to be **subordinate** and happy to serve the bourgeoisie. Marx once said that **religion** is the **opium of the people** — meaning that he thought religion keeps the working class **subdued** and supports a system which works against their interests. Miliband reckons that the mass media is **"the new opium of the people"**.

## *Some Neo-Marxists Say the Ruling Class Indirectly Control Media Content*

In Marxist thought, one of the key powers of the ruling class is the power to **control ideas**, **values** and **attitudes**. The mass media is a useful tool for doing this. The values of the ruling class have dominance in society — this dominance is called **hegemony**.

This theory says that the **ideas** and **values** of the ruling class are **spread** by the mass media, and presented as if they're the most natural, obvious, common sense things to assume and believe.

"The ruling ideas are the ideas of the ruling class."
Marx (1874), *The Communist Manifesto*.

1) Media content is controlled by an **approval process** — articles written by journalists are given the OK by editors. **Editors** are mostly from **white, middle class backgrounds** so they **select content** which **reflects** their own values. The idea is that they do this **unconsciously** — they **don't even realise that they're doing it**. Which is a bit odd and a bit scary. (Journalists also tend to come from middle class backgrounds — that's who newspapers and broadcasters tend to employ.)
2) Some events are given **less media coverage**, and some are **left out completely**. Marxists believe that the media are **trained** to present a **certain view of the world**. This view becomes natural and "obvious" to them and the audience. Neither the media nor the audience are conscious that the media are pushing a certain view. For example, the **royal family** get a lot of coverage and they're usually treated with **respect** by the media.
3) This neo-Marxist view doesn't say that **alternative** views are **suppressed** — it says they're **allowed**. This gives the impression that all views get a fair shout — which makes it seem OK and perfectly fair for the dominant view to stay on top. Alternative views are often made to look silly or immature.
4) Marxist sociologists say the control of ideas **doesn't just happen in news** or factual programmes. For example, family entertainment programmes are presented as light-hearted fun but they present a specific **idea of British family life**.

Gerald liked to get good press.

**Critics of Marxism** don't think all journalists think the same way, and they point out that not all media stories are covered from the same viewpoint.

They also say that the media doesn't always reflect the opinions of the dominant class. For example, the BBC reports of government evidence of weapons of mass destruction in the war with Iraq in 2003 undermined those in power rather than supporting them.

**Pluralists** point out that media audiences aren't completely stupid, and don't all believe everything they see on TV and read in the papers.

# Theories about Mass Media

## **Pluralism** — *Media Content* **Reflects Diversity of Society**

The Pluralist view is that society is made up of lots of **different** and **interacting** parts and the state oversees them to keep them in check. Pluralists think that the **content of the media reflects the values of society**. The **free market economy** is the key to a pluralist media — any media which reflects the values in society will be **popular** and stay in business, any that doesn't will go ti... er, bosoms up. This is how pluralist theory says the media **regulates itself**.

Pluralists point out that the media will express **some opinions more than others**. Pluralists reckon this isn't because of bias from journalists, editors or owners — it's only a reflection of the **most common** views in society.

### Nick Jones (1986) studied reporting of strikes

Jones studied the reporting on **industrial disputes** by the **UK media**. He concluded there was balanced and equal reporting. Individual reports may have been biased but the overall picture was **neutral**. He said apparent bias was down to the opposing sides managing to get good media coverage — the media were happy to publicise any relevant view.

Pluralism is criticised for **assuming** the diversity and neutrality of the mass media and **not showing evidence** for it.

Critics of pluralism point out that studies are often **carried out by people who work in the media**. Jones is a BBC Radio news journalist. This means that the research **might not be impartial**.

### Katz and Lazarsfeld (1955) studied media before a US election

They wanted to find out how much the **media** influenced people's **political opinions** and votes. They concluded that the influence of the media is rather **unpredictable** and is often severely **limited**. They believed it was difficult to influence people through the media. People don't all get exposed to media messages, and don't always pay attention. People's attitudes can completely distort their understanding of a message. People also paid more attention to what their spouse, parents, co-workers and friends said than what the media said.

There's more on this on page 44.

## **Postmodernism** — *Media Content Gives Society a* **Consumerist Identity**

1) Postmodernism says that **consumption** is **more important** than **class** identity. It sees Marxist views about economic power as irrelevant nowadays.
2) Postmodernism says that people's **identity** comes from **what they buy** and what kind of **culture and media** they **choose to consume**. Postmodernists think the media has a very important part to play in **showing people what they can buy** and what kind of **lifestyles** they can choose from.
3) French postmodernist **Baudrillard** says that society is **media-saturated** and full of lots of different images. He believes that audiences merge what they see in the media with their own experiences to make their own individual sense of reality.
4) Postmodernists also say that there's no dominant set of ideas — **no dominant ideology**.

Many sociologists don't trust postmodernism because it's mainly theoretical — there's not much evidence to support it.

## *Practice Questions*

Q1 What is hegemony?

Q2 What do traditional Marxists think advertising is for?

Q3 Why do Neo-Marxists think that alternative, anti-establishment views are allowed on TV and in the papers?

Q4 What do Pluralists think regulates the media?

**Exam Question**

Q1 Identify and explain two criticisms of the Marxist view of the relationship between media and audience. (8 marks)

## *CGP — subconsciously disseminating Cumbrian values since 1995...*

*Hmm. Subtle. Anyway, the big difference between Marxist and Pluralist views is whether the media controls the audience or whether the audience controls the media. You've got traditional Marxists, who think the media's all about making profits for capitalism, and you've got Neo-Marxists who say it passes on ruling class values without even meaning to.*

# Selecting and Presenting the News

*Sociologists have studied the news as an example of how the media works because it reaches so many people. It's the main source of information on the World for most of the population. The news is a social product full of ideas and values — it's not an objective reality out there waiting to be discovered by journalists.*

## *News is Influenced by Practical Constraints — Time, Space and Money*

The news is **presented** to us as the most **factual**, **objective** form of media — the reporting of what's happened in the World that day. In reality, newspapers, radio and television run to very tight **deadlines** and **constraints** which **influence** what finally appears as the news.

1) **Time constraints** mean the most **easily available stories** make it onto the TV/radio news or newspaper. Editors and journalists have **contacts** they use **again and again** for convenience, meaning a **limited number of viewpoints** are used. Also, all news organisations have a "news diary" of regular events. This means they can plan coverage of regular events in advance.
2) **Technical constraints** influence the news. Some places are **easier** to get **cameras**, **microphones** and **journalists** into and these are the places **top stories** will tend to come from. A story will rise and fall in significance **partly** on **how easy it is to report**.
3) News organisations all run to a **budget**. Stories and reports from **places where they already have reporters** or **established contacts** are **cheaper to produce**.
4) Many newspapers **can't afford** to have **many reporters** of their own so they **buy stories from news agencies**. These agencies then have a **huge influence** over what becomes news.

This can lead to, for example, disasters in far-flung places being ignored or under-reported.

It's common these days for celebrities, politicians and groups in society to issue a **press release**. Press releases give the story **straight to the newsroom**, which makes it much more likely to be used because it **saves time and money**.

Also remember stories have to shrink or expand to **fit the space available**. The same story could be on page two one day and page seventeen the next, depending on **what else has happened** or what else is available to report.

Big hint — key studies to use in an exam answer are **Cohen and Young (1981)** *The Manufacture of News* and **Grossberg et al (1998)** *Media making*. Both refer to all of the above as common practices in the media.

## *News is Influenced by Values and Practices of Journalists*

Journalists who report the news learn to follow **certain rules** and ideas, which tend to be based on what they believe the general public want to hear about. Sociologists have referred to these as "**news values**". There are different types of news values which influence the type of news the media chooses to report.

**Bureaucratic news values:**

News should be **current**.
News should be **simple**.
News should be **brief**.
**Big news** is better than **small** news.

**Cultural news values:**

News should be **unexpected**.
News should focus on **important people**.
News should be **relevant to the audience**.
**Bad news** is preferred to **good news**.

The relative importance of the different news values to an individual journalist will depend partly on the type of publication or programme they work for.

Two key practices used by journalists which you must know are **Agenda-setting** and **Gate-keeping**.

### Agenda-setting

**Journalists** and **editors** "control the news agenda". News **only becomes news** when **journalists** and **editors select it** as news. When a story is selected, journalists choose what **angle** to take when reporting it. This has a **direct effect** on how the audience will **perceive** the story. Agenda-setting may not be **conscious**. It comes from **learnt practices** of journalism — usually based on what **catches the audience's attention**.

### Gate-keeping

This comes from work by **Gans (1974)** which describes how the editor decides **which stories are featured** and **how much space** is given to each story. Gans says it's like a gate — the editor opens it for some stories and closes it for others. **Dutton (1986)** concluded from his research: "editors fulfil a filtering role since there is usually an excess of material available to fill limited newspaper or broadcasting space".

# Selecting and Presenting the News

## *Case Study of Selection and Presentation of News*

### The Glasgow University Media Group studied television news

The Glasgow University Media Group (GUMG) studied **television news** over a long time-span (1970s and 1980s) to look for evidence of bias. They focused in particular on coverage of workplace **strikes**. They used **detailed content analysis of television news bulletins**.

| Findings | | Examples |
|---|---|---|
| The **selection of news** was biased in favour of dominant class values. | → | **Picket line violence** was **reported more** than police violence. |
| The **voice-overs** were biased in favour of dominant class values. | → | Words such as "**trouble-makers**" and "**pointless strike**" were used as though they were **neutral**. |
| Management were given **more access** to the media than striker leaders. | → | Television interviews with management were **more frequent** and longer than those with strike leaders. |
| The **filming** and **editing** was biased in favour of the police. | → | Cameras were often placed **behind police lines** showing the police viewpoint. |

The work of the Glasgow University Media Group is used to demonstrate **bias in the news** and in the **values and assumptions** of the individuals who **produce** and **construct** the news. Their work is **highly respected** because they've studied **a lot of news** in **great detail**. Remember though, the work was done in the 1970s so think before you start blithely applying it to the news in 2004.

The **image** of the news as objective reporting of fact makes this bias more **important** and more **powerful**. Because people **think the news is unbiased**, they're **more likely to believe it**.

## *News is Influenced by Society — it's Socially Constructed*

All media sociologists agree the **news is socially constructed** but they disagree over whose values are behind the social construction of news — those of the **dominant class** or those of the **majority of society**.

1) From a **pluralist** perspective, **practical constraints** are more significant in influencing the content of the news than ideological bias. The values of journalists are the **common values in society**.

2) From the **Marxist** perspective, the **ideological influences** are most important, and practical constraints can't be separated from ideology. Journalistic values are part of the **dominant ruling class ideology**.

## *Practice Questions*

Q1 How does money influence the presentation of the news? Give two examples.

Q2 Describe what is meant by "news values".

Q3 Explain how the process of gate-keeping takes place in news production.

Q4 How might the news be said to be 'socially constructed'?

**Exam Question**

Q1 Journalists create rather than discover the news. Discuss. (20 marks)

## *It's funny how the World's events always exactly fill the newspaper...*

*You think you know what news is, and then you read these pages. Suddenly, you know a lot more about news, but it isn't so clear cut any more. News is as much of a social construct as anything else. People choose what to put in the papers and on the telly, and people aren't unbiased and neutral — they're affected by all sorts of factors, and all sorts of ideas.*

# Media Stereotypes

*The role of the media in representing social groups is very influential. These pages look at the images of particular social groups, how they're formulated and what effect they might have.*

## Stereotypes are Inaccurate Generalisations

Stereotypes are **generalisations** about **social groups**. They are **inaccurate** and often **derogatory** — e.g. "Women can't read maps", "Gay men are camp", "Chinese women are submissive."

## Media Messages Go Through Four Stages from Production to End Effect

In "sociology speak" this is called the **process of message trajectory**.

**Stage 1 — Media Message is formulated by editors**

Media messages are **formulated** (put together) by those in **powerful positions** in media institutions. These individuals aren't usually members of the social groups which the media stereotypes. For example, very few media editors are female, disabled, black, working class, openly gay, under 25 or over 65.

**Stage 2 — Media Message content reflects groups in power**

The content of the media **reflects the values** of the people who **formulate** it. Groups who aren't in power have **limited representation** in the media.

**Stage 3 — Media Message is received by the audience**

The messages are then **received** by the audience and **interpreted** in different ways — depending on **context** and **experience**.

**Stage 4 — Media Message affects the role and treatment of social groups**

Opinions and behaviour of **individuals** and **institutions** in society are **influenced** by **messages in the media**. The **impact of the media** depends on how you view the **interaction between media and audience**. It's all very theoretical.

There's plenty of detail about this on pages 44-47.

You need to **know these four stages** and to be able to give **examples** for the **social groups on this page and the following three pages** (gender stereotypes, class stereotypes, disability stereotypes, ethnic stereotypes, age stereotypes and sexuality stereotypes). You can choose other groups but you'd need to **do your own research** to find your own examples.

## Media Messages About Women Are Stereotyped

1) Most **editors** are **men**. Research by **Croteau and Hoynes (2000)** gives evidence for this. They found that in the mid 1990s in the US only 6% of top newspaper management were women and only 20% of top TV management. Women wrote 19% of front page stories and presented 20% of TV news reports.
2) Women **don't appear in the media as often as men**. A Broadcasting Standards Council survey by **Guy Cumberbatch (1990)** found 90% of all advertising voice-overs were male and 66% of all people in adverts were male. Also, women in ads were likely to be young, blonde and not to appear in a workplace setting.
3) Women in the media are often presented as **ideals** for other women to aspire to. **Naomi Woolf (1990)** and **Susan Orbach (1991)** both reckon that the rise in eating disorders in women is a direct result of distorted and idealised images of women's bodies in the media.
4) The media tends to portray women in a limited range of roles. **Tuchman (1978)** argued there were only two female roles portrayed in the media: **domestic** and **sexual**.
5) Women in the media are often presented in a way to **appeal to men** — as attractive, well-groomed and sexy.
6) Women are often represented as **victims** by the media — of sexual violence, domestic violence etc.

**Ferguson (1983)** looked at a wide range of **women's magazines**. She found the magazines gave **advice and training** on **being feminine**. She called this a "cult of femininity" which **reinforced stereotypes** of women as **sexual**, **domestic** and **romantic**. **McRobbie (1978)** studied **teenage girl's magazines**. She concluded that the **main theme** of the magazines was **how to get a boyfriend** — how to be attractive to men.

Postmodernist **Hermes (1995)** thinks people respond to images and stereotypical portrayal of women in a **variety** of ways. Individuals can **reject media messages** in the light of other knowledge and experience they have — people aren't all easily led.

# Media Stereotypes

## Some Sociologists Say There Are *Class Stereotypes* in the Media

1) **Editors** are almost all **middle class**. **Journalists** are often hired partly on the basis of whether their "face fits", so they're usually from the **same middle class background** as the editors.
2) **Middle class** people **appear on TV** more often than working class people, both on **dramas** and on **news** programmes.
3) **Drama roles** for working class characters are mostly limited to **soap operas**. **Upper class** characters are often seen in **historical costume dramas** — which tend to give a **romantic** picture of life and class.
4) In the **news**, **working class** people are often represented as a **source of trouble** — trade union unrest, strikes, crime, vandalism, "anti-social behaviour", etc.

### Glennon and Butsch (1982) looked at TV in the USA

Glennon and Butsch carried out a massive research project into 40 years of family programmes on American TV.

They found that only **4% of sitcoms** featured a family where the head of the household was a **manual worker**. In real life, **36%** of American families were like this.

Nearly **half** the **TV families** had a **professional** as head of the household. In real life, only 25% were like this.

Most of the families were wealthy and glamorous.

Glennon and Butsch thought that most **working class dads** were portrayed as **stupid** and **comical**, for the audience to laugh at.

This is their opinion though, not necessarily the opinion of the actual TV audience.

"Look," said Saskia. "Do you see what I see?" "Golly," said Rupert. "Working class people on the telly. Whatever will they think of next?"

**Stuart Hall (1982, 1992, 1996)** thinks that the media has always portrayed the **middle classes** in a **positive** light and the **working class** in a **negative** light. He says that the media has reinforced people's class identities — which keeps the divide between the classes going strong.

**Ann Gray (1992)** looked at how women from different social classes used TV and video.
She found that **working class women** watched a lot **more TV** and video.
Women in **higher social classes** had a strong preference for "classic" and "quality" programmes.

## Practice Questions

Q1 Write a summary of the four stages of a media message in no more than four sentences.

Q2 Give two examples of social groups which have been identified as being subject to stereotyped media portrayal.

Q3 List two pieces of research which illustrate the argument that the media is a patriarchal institution.

Q4 Describe how Glennon and Butsch (1982) conducted their research and explain what their findings were.

**Exam Questions**

Q1 With reference to sociological studies, assess the view that the mass media is biased in its portrayal of women. (20 marks)

Q2 How does social class play a role in the construction of stereotyped images in the mass media? (20 marks)

## *Learn the studies, you'll need them...*

*Remember, it's not just women who are stereotyped by the media. Men are also portrayed in a limited way, which tends to be as a strong, capable breadwinner. Dramas which contain violence generally portray men as the aggressors, and they're more likely to be shown as criminals too. So, if a question asks about gender stereotypes, remember to talk about men as well as women.*

# Media Stereotypes

*The media sends out stereotypes about disabled people, ethnic minorities, young people, old people and gay people. That's a lot of people.*

## *Disabled* People are *Under-represented* in the Media

1) Disabled people are **poorly represented** in **powerful positions** in the media. Those who do hold powerful positions tend to have specialised in disabled issues — e.g. Peter White, the radio journalist.
2) There's really **very little representation of disabled people** in the media at all. Government statistics show that about 20% of the adult population has some form of disability, yet the Broadcasting Standards Commission (1999) reported that people with disabilities only appeared in **7% of television programmes** and had only **0.75% of all speaking roles.**
3) **Roles** for disabled people are very **limited**. Research by **Cumberbatch and Negrine (1992)** looking at British television over six weeks found the roles for disabled people were based on **pity** or **comedy**. They found that **disabled actors** never appeared **just as actors** playing a person who **just happened to have a disability**, only in **roles particularly about disability**. However, there are **some positive portrayals** of disabled people in films and on TV — e.g. *Four Weddings and a Funeral.*
4) **Audience response** depends on people's **actual experience** of disability. Cumberbatch and Negrine researched audience responses as part of their study. They concluded that people with limited or **no real life experience** of disability **accepted** the media images with **little concern**.
People **with experience** of disability were **critical** of the media and **rejected** stereotyped images.

## Media Representations of *Ethnicity* are *Stereotyped*

1) New technology means there are more satellite and digital TV channels. Lots of small specialised channels have developed. Many of these **cater for specific ethnic minorities** and they're managed and controlled by people from those ethnic minorities (e.g. Zee TV, Bangla TV, Punjabi TV).
2) However, there aren't many people from ethnic minorities in positions of **power** in **mainstream media**. Have a good look at the difference between this and point 1. Ethnic minorities are **marginalised** in the media — shunted off into non-mainstream **specialist** media organisations.
3) There aren't very many **roles** played by members of **ethnic minorities** on TV. For example, a study of **American TV** by **Greenberg et al (1983)** found **97%** of characters on daytime soaps and dramas were white and **87%** of characters on primetime soaps and dramas were white. This is starting to change though.
4) Roles for ethnic minorities are often **stereotyped** and **limited**. **Stuart Hall (1982)** said that **in the past** there were three main stereotypes: **slave, "native" and entertainer**. Remember that Hall was talking about the past, not the present. Ethnic minority characters in soap operas are getting **less stereotyped** — e.g. characters on EastEnders.
5) There's evidence that ethnic minorities are presented **negatively** in the papers — as criminals, as illegal immigrants, as terrorists or as victims of famine. **Van Dijk (1991)** made a detailed analysis of **headlines** in five British national newspapers. He found **negative images** far outweighed positive images in all five papers. It's well worth your while learning a couple of statistics from this table of his results:

| **Newspaper** | The Times | The Telegraph | The Guardian | The Mail | The Sun |
|---|---|---|---|---|---|
| **Negative image of ethnic minority** | 19 | 32 | 14 | 16 | 25 |
| **Positive image of ethnic minority** | 4 | 4 | 5 | 4 | 1 |

6) **Audience response** to ethnic minority stereotypes varies depending on the **real life experience** of the audience. People don't swallow media stereotypes if they know better themselves.

**Maria Gillespie** looked at how **Punjabi teenagers** responded to **British TV** from 1988 to 1991. She concluded that the media gave teenagers the opportunity to **compare** Punjabi culture with **Western** culture.

**Hartmann and Husband (1974) analysed children's response to media**

They compared the responses of children in two parts of Britain and found that in the **area with low ethnic mix**, children **believed negative media content** and thought of "race relations" in terms of conflict. In the **area with a high ethnic mix**, children **rejected media stereotypes** in favour of their own experience.

# Media Stereotypes

## *Images of **Young** and **Old** are **Stereotyped** in the Media*

1) The **people with power** in media organisations tend to be **older**. It takes **time** to get **experience**, so this makes sense.
2) There's often a sexist **double standard** in the way older people are represented in the media. The **older** a **woman** gets, the **less likely** she is to get a leading film role or a TV presenting job. It's a different story for men. In films, older male actors like Sean Connery and Harrison Ford are "allowed" to be romantically paired with cute young women. There are lots more **older men presenting TV programmes** than there are older women.
3) **Biggs (1993)** focused on entertainment programmes and found lots of representation of older people. However, they were often in stereotyped roles of "forceful", "vague" and "difficult" — especially in sitcoms. In America, **Signorelli (1989)** studied television characters and found that both young and old were under-represented on prime-time television. TV was biased towards **middle-aged** people.
4) **Featherstone and Hepworth (1995)** found that magazines aimed at older people tended to push an image of "youthful" old people — enjoying holidays and sports, wearing fashionable, "young-looking" clothes, etc.
5) There are also **stereotypes** relating to **young people**. **Children** are represented as **innocent**. Slightly older "**youth**" are often seen as a **social problem** — prone to drug abuse, binge drinking, petty crime and unplanned pregnancy.

**Stan Cohen (1973)** first used the term "**moral panic**" to describe how **media reporting** of expected "trouble" could **create panic** in society.

Small group behaves in a deviant way → Media report the story → Media report similar stories again → Original group labelled as threat to social order → More people join in with deviant behaviour → Moral panic — public demands that something is done about it

Cohen used the example of the **Mods and Rockers** in the 1960s. The media reported that there would be **fights** between two youth subcultures — the Mods and the Rockers. Lots of people turned up to fight or watch, partly because of the **media publicity**. The public then **panicked** over reports of how many people turned up to fight.

You can easily find **contemporary** examples of a moral panic — e.g. the concern over trouble at **So Solid Crew** gigs. The possibility of **gun violence** led to some shows being cancelled because **media reporting** of the concern led to **panic**.

## *Representations of **Sexuality** in the Media are **Stereotyped***

1) Gay men are often stereotyped as "**camp**". TV shows often use "camp" gay characters as **comic relief**.
2) Homosexual relationships and heterosexual relationships are shown differently in the media. For example, much more explicit heterosexual sex is shown on television than homosexual sex. **Coronation Street** and **EastEnders** have both had storylines involving a **gay kiss** which got widespread media attention. You don't get any outcry in the papers when a **man and a woman** kiss on a soap opera.
3) There was a **political** aspect to early **media reporting** of **HIV/AIDS**. It was initially openly characterised as a "gay disease". A *Daily Mail* headline in the 1980s referred to AIDS as a "gay plague".

## *Practice Questions*

Q1 Briefly explain the findings of Cumberbatch and Negrine (1992).

Q2 Give an example of newspaper bias in relation to ethnic minorities in Britain.

Q3 How does real-life experience affect how people respond to stereotypes in the media?

**Exam Questions**

Q1 Examine the view that the media are biased in their representation of ethnic minorities. (20 marks)

Q2 With reference to sociological studies, evaluate the claim that the media are ideologically biased. (20 marks)

## *Learn these studies...in fact learn ALL the studies...in the world... EVER...*

*If you do a question on media audiences and ethnicity, disability, age or sexuality, you have to be prepared to mention some sociological studies to back up your points. It's the only way to get the marks. The stuff on these pages makes you think a bit. British society, and the media especially, has a way to go before it treats everyone equally.*

# Mass Media and its Audience

*The media constructs and sends out messages to the public — but the impact of the messages depends on how the audience responds. People can accept media messages, or dismiss them as complete rubbish.*

## *The **Hypodermic Syringe** Theory — Media **Directly Influences Audience***

Way back in the **1920s**, when **radio** and **newspapers** were just starting to get **important** in society, sociologists developed theories about how the media affected people.

1) The **hypodermic syringe theory** says the media **injects** its message into the mind of the audience in the same way as drugs are **directly injected** into the body. The idea is that the media is **so powerful**, its message **directly influences** the individual and they're **powerless** to **resist** the message or **reject** it.
2) This theory says that **all individuals** in the audience are **affected** in the **same way**.

> In **1938**, Orson Welles recorded a radio production of HG Wells' story *The War of the Worlds* in which Martians invade Earth. The broadcast included **fictional news bulletins** reporting the Martian invasion. Some radio listeners **believed** the fake bulletins were true, and **panicked**. This was used as **evidence** of the **dangerous** and **direct power of the media** and it created concern in society. For the hypodermic syringe theorists it was proof enough.

3) Some sociologists decided that the hypodermic syringe theory was **too simplistic** to explain how adults view media content. It did stay popular as a theory of how the **media** can **influence children**, though.
4) **Bandura, Ross and Ross (1963)** played children a **film of a man hitting a doll**. They then left the children to play with the **same doll** which they'd seen on the film. The children who'd seen the violence on film hit the doll. Those who hadn't seen the film played with the doll in a non-violent way.

Critics of the hypodermic syringe theory think it treats people as **passive** and very easily led. They also point out that **not all audience members react in the same way** to the same piece of media. Studies showed this as far back as the 1920s.

> Don't assume that this theory is dead in the water. Think about the **concern** that **fictional TV** and **film violence** can cause violent acts in society. In 1992, two 11 year old boys were convicted of **killing two year old Jamie Bulger** — when the judge was summing up he said that **watching a violent film** was "partly responsible".

## *The Media Message is **Interpreted** and **Passed On** by **Key Individuals***

The **two-step flow model** was developed in the 1950s. It says that the media does influence people, but **not everyone is influenced directly**.

1) The **first step** is the **media message** reaching an audience member. All simple so far.
2) The important **second step** is how their **understanding** of the message is **shaped** by **social interaction** with other audience members. For example, if workers in an office chat about a soap opera during their coffee break then these discussions affect individuals' opinions of the storyline and characters.
3) **Katz and Lazarsfeld (1955)** said that there were **key individuals** in each community whose reaction **directly influenced others**. These "**opinion leaders**" openly expressed their reaction and opinions, and others **followed** their lead. Katz and Lazarsfeld studied **media influence on American voters**. They concluded that most people followed the opinion leader's views on who they should vote for, but the opinion leaders themselves often got their **ideas straight from the mass media** messages.
4) It doesn't have to be just two steps — a message can go through several stages of interpretation. **Hobson (1990)** studied an office environment and found that a few **key individuals** influenced what the others watched on television and their **reactions** to the programmes. These opinions were **passed on** to another bunch of colleagues. A **social norm** of what to watch **spread** through the **whole office**. **New recruits** had to **conform** to fit in.

It's easy to imagine this happening in a school or a workplace: "Did you see Big Brother?" "Isn't she such a COW?" "He loves himself, doesn't he?". If you don't watch the programme, you're left out of the conversation. If you don't agree with the ~~bigmouth~~ opinion leader, you're made to feel a bit of an outsider.

# Mass Media and its Audience

## *Social* and *Cultural Context* Affect how an *Audience Responds* to the *Media*

1) The **Cultural Effects theory** introduced the idea that **social context** is important when looking at the effects of the media. In short, they argued that **different people** interpret the media in **different ways**.
2) The idea is that an audience **interprets the media** in the **context** of the **culture** they already belong to. This means that the effect of the media is quite complex — it's not the same for everyone.
3) "**Culture**" refers to the **small, sub-cultural groups** an individual belongs to and also to the **wider, general culture of society**. For example, in England an individual's response to Arsenal winning the Premiership will **depend** on whether the **individual** supports Arsenal or not. But audience response to media reports of **England winning the World Cup** would be broadly **similar** because there's a **cultural norm** of supporting your country's sports teams.

Here's a **second look** at the audience response to the *War of the Worlds* broadcast — this time from a **Cultural Effects viewpoint (Cantril, 1940)**.

1) The response was **caused** by the **cultural context** in which it was heard. If it was on the radio **today** it wouldn't create the same response.
2) At the time of the broadcast there was **insecurity** in American society because of a **financial crisis** and the move towards **war in Europe**. Radio programmes were **frequently interrupted for news reports**, and there was a general expectation of bad news.
3) People **wouldn't have been surprised** to hear a **real report** of bad news interrupting a drama programme on the radio. This made it **more likely** that some members of the audience would **believe** the story.

## *The Effects of Media Messages* **Build Up Over Time**

1) The Cultural Effects theory made sociologists look at the **long term effects** of the media.
2) Media effects build up over time to **create** or **reinforce** cultural **norms**.
3) For example, **images of women** in the media create **stereotypical images** and place **expectations** on girls and women. There's been a long-running campaign by some feminists to remove pictures of **topless women** ("Page Three Girls") from national newspapers, because they argue that these images reinforce the dominant view that it's OK to objectify women as sex objects.

## *Practice Questions*

Q1 Briefly explain the hypodermic syringe theory.

Q2 In which study did sociologists show children a film of a person hitting a doll?

Q3 Define the two steps in the two-step flow model.

Q4 Explain what's meant by the term "opinion leader".

Q5 Briefly explain Cultural Effects theory.

Q6 Name the sociologist who did a study of *The War of the Worlds* panic in 1940.

**Exam Questions**

Q1 Evaluate the claim that audiences are passive in their response to media messages, with reference to at least two sociological theories. (20 marks)

Q2 "The hypodermic syringe model is outdated." Discuss. (20 marks)

## *The Hypodermic Syringe theory — it gets right under your skin...*

*You read one theory and think "ah, that explains it", then you read the next theory and think "ah, that explains it" — and they're two totally contradictory theories, so they can't both be right. I suppose they can both be right some of the time, or they can give you a part of the picture. The most important thing is that you can write about them in the exam.*

# Mass Media and its Audience

*Here's more about how people interpret what they see and hear from the mass media.*
*Some sociologists think people can be quite active in deciding what media messages they want to see and hear.*

## *Audiences **Actively Use** and **Interpret** the Media to **Suit Their Own Needs***

There's a bunch of media theories which are grouped together as "**interpretive theories**".
They all argue that the audience responds **actively** to media content and messages.
There's a switch from "what the **media** does **to** people" to "what **people** do **with** the media".

### Uses and Gratifications Theory

1) This theory was developed in the **1960s** by **Blumler and Katz**. It says that people **use** the media to **meet their needs**. The audience **actively chooses** what media to experience, using such cutting edge tools as free will and the remote control. Everyone chooses for themselves, so each person's media diet is **unique**.
2) A good example is the study of **soap opera audiences** by **McQuail (1972)**. He looked at how audiences used **Coronation Street** to fulfil a need for **social companionship**. Audiences felt part of the characters' lives and felt interest and concern for what would happen next in a storyline.
3) **Lull (1990)** listed the social uses of television in the UK — and found men, women, young and old all used the media to meet different needs.
4) Uses and Gratification Theory is **functionalist** — it says the media exists to serve the **needs** of the public.

In media language, "to engage with" a piece of media means to find it interesting and pay attention to it — to be "into" it.

### Selective Filter Model

1) This theory says the audience **choose** which media to **experience** and also **control** which parts of the media message to listen to and **engage with**. The audience pick out the parts of a message which **fit in with their view of the world** and **ignore the rest**.
2) **Fiske (1988)** says individuals become very **experienced readers of the media**. He says that individuals can understand one "**media text**" in several **different ways** on several **different levels** — and in relation to **other** "**media texts**" on the same subject.
3) Here's an example to make it clear: when watching a **TV drama series**, you can get **caught up in the fictional drama**, and at the same time **know a character is going to die** because you read it in a **newspaper article** about the series. Or you might like a character because he's played by an actor you liked in another TV series. This is called an "**intertextual response**" in the exciting language of media sociology.
4) This model emphasises the **power of the individual** to control his / her experience of the media and says that people use media in a **sophisticated** way. It's kinda postmodern in that way. However, it's been criticised for **overestimating** the control of the individual over very **powerful media messages**.

"Media text" means a piece of media — a TV programme, a newspaper article, a magazine article, an advert. Academics really like to call things "texts" for some reason. Oh well, if it makes them happy...

### Structured Interpretation Model

1) This theory says there's a **dominant interpretation** of media messages which audiences go along with. Like the other two theories, individuals actively **pick** which media they **engage with**, but this theory says the process takes place in a **social context**. The social context creates a "**preferred reading**" of the media message (by "reading" they mean "interpretation"). For example a film is written, presented and promoted with a **preferred reading** in mind — the makers of a film like *Cold Mountain* want you to find the love story **moving** and **tragic**, not stilted and laughable.
2) **Different social groups** have **different dominant interpretations** of the same text. So, this theory isn't the same as earlier theories which saw the audience as a mass who all respond in the same way.
3) **Morley (1980)** studied how the television audience responded to one **news programme** — *Nationwide*. He showed the same programme to several **different social groups** and found that their responses to the programme **varied** hugely between groups **but within each group** most **individuals responded in the same way**. Trade unionists saw it as biased towards management, but management trainees saw it as pro-union.

# Mass Media and its Audience

## **Postmodernism** Says the Audience Gets **Lots of Meanings**

1) **Postmodernists** say that there are **many**, **many meanings** to any social or cultural aspect of life. They say there **isn't any aspect of life** where there's one single, objective **truth** or **reality** that absolutely everyone experiences. That's a really important part of postmodernism.
2) Another important fact about postmodernism is that it can **make your head swim** if you try to think about it too hard. Just warning you because I care...

> **Baudrillard (1988)** says that the development of the media and technological advances have meant everyday life is **chock-full of images** and messages all competing and **conflicting** with each other. Audiences experience all these messages alongside each other — leading to a state he calls **hyperreality** where **no single word** or **image** has a **straightforward meaning**. *Whoah*. Like, *dude*. Seriously, whoah.

3) The media presents so many different **images** and **stories** which have been **woven into everyday life** that the **boundary** between **reality** and the **media** is **blurred**.

> **Turkle (1996)** reckons that individuals can relate to a **simulated world** as easily as **reality** — the characters in the pretend world become significant in their own right. The explosion of **reality TV** and the **obsessive interest** people have with **soap stars** are good examples of this. With **reality TV**, **real** people get put in an **unreal situation** which is presented as **real**, and the audience follows it like a **soap**. With a soap, **pretend** characters get treated by the press and by audiences **as if they're real**. So it's real, not real, real, not real and real again. At the same time. Again, *whoah*.

### Conclusions of Postmodernism

1) The **conclusion** from postmodern theory is that the media is not only **complex** and **interactive** but it actually **isn't concrete or definite**.
2) There's **no one dominant message** or truth which is being conveyed — there's a range of **varying realities** for the **individual** to **interpret**.
3) This suits the idea of the **postmodern audience** who don't follow one clear path through life but **pick** and **choose** between a range of opportunities and alternatives.

## **Critics** say Postmodernism's too **Theoretical**

1) **Postmodernism is criticised for being too theoretical**. It's really **hard to find** (or even think of) any kind of **evidence** which would **prove** postmodernism **right** or **wrong**. I mean, if you're starting out from the premise that no idea has a straightforward meaning, and individuals create their own reality so that there is no one definition of what is "real" or "true" — *where on earth do you go from there...*
2) **Postmodernism** doesn't acknowledge that there's **inequality** in society and in the media. In real life, **not all messages**, views or "realities" **ever get presented** by the media.

## Practice Questions

Q1 What do sociologists mean when they refer to an audience actively responding to the media content?

Q2 Explain the term "preferred reading" in relation to the media.

Q3 Explain why *Big Brother* is a good example of postmodern TV.

Q4 Give two criticisms of postmodern ideas about mass media audiences.

**Exam Questions**

Q1 Compare and contrast the differing models of audience response known as interpretive theories. (20 marks)

Q2 "Media audiences actively select and filter the content and messages they receive". Discuss. (20 marks)

## Whenever I fancy feeling like I've shoved my head in a blender...

*... with an Amazon tree frog and a shot of ouzo, I read some postmodernism. There is kind of a point behind it, though. If you limit it to "people pick and choose what they believe" and "people think things are real when they're not really" it's not too bad. Having said that, I dare you to read Jacques Lacan or Jacques Derrida. I double dog dare you.*

# The Role of the Education System

*Different theories try to explain the role or function of education in society. Some of them look at the positive functions. Some look at how education oppresses pupils and maintains inequality. Some look at pupil interaction in the classroom. Some say we should get rid of school altogether... Yay.*

## ***Functionalism** Says Education Has **Three Functions** that Help Society*

1) Education teaches the **skills** needed in **work** and by the **economy**.
2) Education **sifts and sorts people** for the **appropriate jobs**. This is called the **allocation** function.
3) Education plays a part in **secondary socialisation**, passing on **core values**.

1) **Durkheim** said that education passes on **norms** and **values** in order to **integrate** individuals into society. Education helps to **create social order** based on cohesion and value **consensus**.
2) **Parsons** describes school as a bridge between the family and adult roles of society. Schools pass on a **universal value** of **achievement**. Parsons says that education **selects** children for **appropriate roles** because it's **meritocratic** (meaning that the best students rise to the top). He agrees with Durkheim that education helps to make people agree about norms and values.
3) **Davis and Moore (1945)** say that every society sorts its members into different positions. They think that there are **rules** for how education does this — called "**principles of stratification**". They believe that there has to be a system of **unequal rewards** (more money or status) to **motivate** people to train for the top positions.

The **functionalist** perspective says that education is **meritocratic**. A **meritocracy** is when social **rewards** are allocated by **talent** and **effort** rather than being **born** into a position.

**Talent + motivation + equal opportunity = qualifications and a high position in society**

## ***Marxism** Says **Education Legitimises Inequality** through **Ideology***

1) Education **prepares children** for the **world of work** by giving them **skills** and **values** they'll need.
2) Education **justifies inequality**.
3) Education passes on **ruling class ideology** that **supports capitalism**.

1) The neo-Marxist **Althusser** sees education as part of the "ideological state apparatus". In other words, it's a tool of capitalism which is used to pass on the belief that society is fair. Althusser thinks education produces a **docile and obedient workforce**.
2) **Bowles and Gintis (1976)** say that there is a close link between school and work. They say that there's a **correspondence** between **pupil experiences of school** and **adult work**:
   - Pupils are taught to accept the **hierarchy** at school. Work also has a **hierarchy**.
   - Pupils are **motivated by grades** to do **boring work**. Workers are **rewarded with pay** to do **boring work**.
   - Both the **school day** and **work day** are split into units (e.g. before and after lunch).
   - At school and work, **subservience** (following the rules) is **rewarded**.

   Bowles and Gintis say that the "**hidden curriculum**" (things like being on time for lessons, and doing your homework) **prepares people for work**. They also say that meritocracy is a **myth** which is used to **blame people** for not succeeding.
3) **Willis (1977)** says that education **doesn't turn out** an **obedient workforce**. Some kids form an **anti-school subculture** and cope with school and then adult work by mucking about.
4) **Bourdieu** used the concept of **cultural capital** (language, skills, knowledge and attitudes) to explain how the middle class get into the top positions. There's **plenty** on this on pages 50-51.

## ***Radicals** like **Illich** Want to **Get Rid Of School Completely***

**Illich (1971)** believes that education has four functions:

Illich agrees with functionalists about the functions of school — but he thinks the functions aren't good enough. So we should give up school as a bad idea.

1) Education **looks after kids** during the day.
2) Education **sorts pupils into job roles**.
3) Education **passes on dominant values**.
4) Education helps people learn **skills and knowledge**.

The problem for Illich is that schools **don't create equality** or **develop creativity**. Illich wants to "**deschool society**". He wants everyone to have **access to education throughout their lives** according to what they need.

# The Role of the Education System

## There are Problems with Functionalist and Marxist Views

### Criticisms of Functionalism

1) Evidence of **differential achievement**, in terms of class, gender and ethnicity suggests that education is **not meritocratic**.
2) "**Who you know**" is still more important than "what you know" in some parts of society. So the allocation function isn't working properly.
3) It can be argued that the education system **doesn't prepare people** adequately for **work**. For example, the dearth of engineering graduates indicates education is failing to produce what **employers** and the **economy** need.
4) Functionalism doesn't look at how education may serve the interests of particular groups in terms of **ideology** and **values**. It **doesn't explain conflict**.

### Criticisms of Marxism

1) Marxism assumes people are **passive victims**. It **exaggerates** how much working class students are **socialised** into **obedience**. Willis showed how students actually resist authority.
2) Most people are **aware of the inequality** in education. Most people don't believe that society is fair.

The problem with both approaches is that they don't look at interaction and social processes within the school.

## There are Similarities and Differences Between Functionalist and Marxist Views

1) Both Functionalism and Marxism look at the **big picture** — institutions and the whole structure of society. They tend to **ignore social interaction** — with the exception of Willis. Both say education has a **huge impact** on the individual and that there's a **close link** with the **economy** and **work**.
2) The biggest **difference** is how they see **inequality**. Marxists say education helps to **maintain inequality** and **make people accept inequality**. Functionalists say education passes on the value of **meritocracy** and lets people **better themselves**.

## Feminists say that the Education System is Patriarchal

1) Some feminists argue that the hidden curriculum unofficially **reinforces gender differences**.
2) There are still **gender differences** in **subject choice** in schools. Gender stereotyping may still exist.
3) Girls are now outperforming boys at school — but **boys** still **demand more attention** from the teacher.
4) **Men** seem to dominate the top positions in schools (**head teacher**, **deputy head**) and even more so in universities.

**Marxist** feminists want to consider gender inequalities **combined with inequalities** of **class** and **ethnicity**.
**Radical** feminists believe men are a bad influence, and want **female-centred education** for girls.
**Liberal** feminists want **equal access to education for both sexes**.

## Practice Questions

Q1 According to Functionalists, what three functions does the education system perform?
Q2 Name two functionalist studies of education.
Q3 What is meant by meritocracy?
Q4 What did Bowles and Gintis say education had a close correspondence with?
Q5 Give two problems with the Marxist theory of education.
Q6 What is the main difference between Marxist and Functionalist approaches to education?

**Exam Question**

Q1 Assess the Marxist view that the function of the education system is to pass on ideology and reproduce the existing class structure. (20 marks)

## Getting rid of school sounds good, but what'd you have instead?

*Mmm, there's lots of theory here. If you know what Marxism, Functionalism and Feminism are, then their views of school **shouldn't come as a big shock**. Functionalists think education brings social harmony. Marxists say school is there to produce an obedient workforce. Feminists think school reinforces gender inequality and difference. They're so predictable.*

# Class and Differential Achievement in Education

*Sociologists have investigated how social class affects how well people do at school. Financial and cultural factors are studied, as well as in-school factors like streaming.*

## Social Class tends to Affect Educational Achievement

I wonder if class affects how well you do in a school of fish...

1) Pupils from **professional** backgrounds are significantly **more likely** to enter **higher education** than those from unskilled backgrounds.
2) Pupils from **middle class** backgrounds are more likely to study **A-Levels**, whereas **working class** pupils are more likely to take **vocational** subjects.
3) Pupils from disadvantaged backgrounds are **more likely** to **leave school at 16** and **less likely** to start school being able to **read**.
4) Pupils from **unskilled backgrounds** on average achieve **lower scores** on SATs and in GCSEs and are more likely to be placed in **lower streams** or **bands**.

Some sociologists have suggested the relative intelligence levels of different socio-economic and ethnic groups accounts for discrepancies in educational attainment (**Eysenck (1971)** and others). But it is difficult to isolate whether IQ or social factors are the key to determining educational achievement.

## Processes Inside School — Labelling, Streaming and Subcultures are Factors

1) **Negative labelling** of students can lead to a **self-fulfilling prophecy of failure**. **Becker (1971)** and **Keddie (1971)** say that teachers tend to evaluate pupils in terms of an **ideal student**, by looking at appearance, personality, speech and social class.
2) Negative labelling can mean students get put into **lower streams or bands**. **Ball (1981)** found that the pupils in the top bands were from **higher social classes**. Teachers had **higher expectations** of them and they were **taught in different ways**. Keddie found that teachers allowed pupils in the top streams access to higher levels of knowledge. Working class students didn't get this knowledge.
3) As a response to negative labelling and frustration with low status, pupils may form **anti-school subcultures**. **Hargreaves (1975)** found that those in the **bottom streams** were more likely to be non-conformist. **Woods (1983)** responded by saying that there are lots of different reactions to school, but **non-conformist** reactions were more likely to come from **working-class** students.

These explanations are useful when looking at day-to-day experiences in schools. The problem is that they don't explain how **factors outside of school** (e.g. poverty, cultural deprivation) can influence achievement.

Labelling theory is also too **deterministic** — it says that once you're negatively labelled that's it, you'll fail. This isn't always the case.

## Material Deprivation Outside School Can Affect Achievement

The theory of **material deprivation** says that **economic poverty** is a big factor in low achievement at school.

1) In 1997, the **Joseph Rowntree Foundation** classified **one in ten** children as **poor** — which was defined as being in a family that couldn't afford at least three things other families took for granted.
2) **Halsey (1980)** found that the **most important factor** preventing working class students staying on at school was **lack of financial support**.
3) **Douglas (1964)** found that children in **unsatisfactory living conditions** (poor housing, lack of nutritious food, overcrowding) didn't do very well in ability tests compared to kids from comfortable backgrounds.
4) **Unemployment** or **low income** means less money for books, the Internet and school trips. Low income families can't afford **nurseries** and **private schools** and they can't afford to support their kids through **uni**.
5) Poverty and unsatisfactory living standards may cause **health problems** and **absence from school**.

## Cultural Deprivation Outside School Can Affect Achievement

The theory of **cultural deprivation** says that **working class culture** and **parenting** aren't aimed at educational success.

1) **Douglas (1964)** thought **level of parental interest** was the most important factor in affecting achievement. Middle class parents are more likely to visit schools for open evenings. Bear in mind that **working class parents** may not go to open evenings because they work **inconvenient shifts** — not because they aren't interested.
2) Some sociologists say that working class kids don't have the **knowledge** and **values** that help achievement. **Museum visits**, **books** and **parental knowledge of education** may help middle class pupils to succeed.
3) Some **styles of parenting** emphasise the importance of education more than others.

# Class and Differential Achievement in Education

## Some Sociologists say **Class Affects Attitudes** to **Education**

1) **Sugarman (1970)** said that pupils from non-manual backgrounds and manual backgrounds have **different outlooks**. The pupils from **manual** backgrounds lived for **immediate gratification** (see p. 6). The pupils from **non-manual backgrounds** were **ambitious** and **deferred their gratification** — they spent time studying and planned for the future.
2) **Hyman (1967)** said that the **values** of the working-class are a **self-imposed barrier** to improving their position. He said that the working-class tend to place a **low value** on education.

ethnocentric = believing your group/nation/culture is superior to others.

**But...**

Material and cultural deprivation theories **don't** explain how **factors inside school** affect achievement.

**Cultural** deprivation theory **generalises a lot** about differences between middle class and working class life. It **ignores** working class families who **do** place a high value on education, and tends to **assume** that working class families have **no culture** at all, or that working class culture can't be **relevant** to school. This is **ethnocentric**.

The **method** may be **unsound**, e.g. attending parents' evenings might not be a good measure of parental interest.

## The Two Bs (**Bernstein** and **Bourdieu**) Investigated **Differences** in **Achievement**

1) **Bernstein (1970)** found that working class pupils in the East End of London weren't comfortable with the style of language required by school. They used a **restricted code** — short forms of speech.
2) **Middle class students** knew how to use the same **elaborated code** as the **teachers** — a much more wordy style of speech with everything made very explicit.
3) In terms of **language**, the working class kids were at a disadvantage.

1) **Bourdieu (1971, 1974)** reckons middle class students are at an advantage because they have the right kind of "**cultural capital**" — the right **language**, **skills**, **knowledge** and **attitudes**.
2) He thought that the **more cultural capital** you have, the **more successful** you'll be in education — and he believed that working class pupils don't have **access** to cultural capital.
3) **Middle class** families **pass on cultural capital** and **expectations** from parents to children. This is called **cultural reproduction**.

| Problems with Bernstein's theory | Problems with Bourdieu's theory |
|---|---|
| There are **variations within** the middle class and working class. Different sections of these groups **vary** in how they use the **elaborated code** — the "posh language" of teachers. | **Halsey (1980)** found that **material factors** are important. **Lack of money** may **stop kids staying on at school** or **getting to university**. |
| Some sociologists have developed his ideas to say working class speech patterns are inferior or somehow "wrong" — controversial... **Labov (1973)** thinks the elaborated speech code is just **different**. | **Not all working-class students fail**, even if they don't have cultural capital. |

## Practice Questions

Q1 Give two facts about social class and educational achievement.

Q2 Name two factors inside school that explain the links between social class and achievement.

Q3 For Halsey, what was the most important factor preventing working class students staying on at school?

Q4 Briefly outline the findings of Sugarman's 1970 research into class attitudes to education.

Q5 Who initially placed an emphasis on the term "cultural capital"?

**Exam Questions**

Q1 (a) Identify and briefly explain two factors in schools that influence working class pupils' levels of achievement. (8 marks)

(b) Assess the view that the home is the major factor in determining different levels of educational achievement between social classes. (20 marks)

## Immediate gratification sounds good to me...

*Just a quick word of warning. In the Exam you could get a question like "Assess how factors inside and outside school affect levels of achievement". This is a very broad question. You'd need to look at home and school factors for ethnicity, gender AND class. This means you'd need to have revised pages 52-55 as well as this page and the previous one.*

# Ethnicity and Differential Achievement in Education

*Ethnicity is another factor that can influence how well people do at school.*
*Quick reminder — ethnicity means the shared cultural traditions and history which are distinct from other groups in society. Modern Britain is said to be a multi-cultural society made up of many different ethnic groups.*

## *Some* ***Ethnic Groups*** *Do* ***Better*** *Than* ***Others***

These figures are from **Modood et al (1997)** — the Policy Studies Institute's fourth survey of ethnic minorities in Britain.

All these statistics are averages. If you look at someone and say "she does well cos she's Chinese" you might be wrong.

### Higher levels of achievement

1) The survey found that **Chinese**, **African Asians** and **Indian** groups were more qualified than whites. **Afro-Caribbean women** were more likely to have **A-levels** than white women.
2) Ethnic minorities were **more likely than white pupils** to continue into **further education** (from ages 16-19).
3) People from ethnic minorities who were **born** in **the UK** had much **higher qualifications** than people who moved to the UK from abroad.

### Lower levels of achievement

1) **Bangladeshi** and **Pakistani women** were least well qualified. **Afro-Caribbean**, **Pakistani** and **Bangladeshi men** were least qualified.
2) **Pakistani** and **Afro-Caribbean** groups were **less likely** to get onto **university** courses, and **more likely** to get into **less prestigious universities**.
3) **Afro-Caribbean boys** are **more likely** to be **excluded from school**, more likely to be put in **lower streams** and more likely to do **vocational** courses.

African Asians means people of Indian origin who lived in Kenya and Uganda and then moved to Britain in the 1970s.

There are big **variations** between the **average achievement level** of different ethnic minority groups. There must be something behind it all — probably more than one factor, and probably some **social** and **economic** factors.

**Some** people say that **intelligence is inherited** — i.e. people underachieve because they've inherited low IQ.

HOWEVER... **IQ tests** can be **biased**. Sometimes they ask things that aren't really a test of brains, but really a test of **cultural knowledge**. The **Swann Report (1985)** found that if you took into account social and economic factors there were **no significant differences in IQ** whatsoever between different **ethnic groups**.

## *Processes Inside School —* ***Labelling****,* ***Curriculum*** *and* ***Prejudice*** *are Factors*

**Labelling theory** says that teachers have **different expectations** of **different ethnic minority groups**. **Gillborn (1990)** found that teachers **negatively label black students**. Afro-Caribbean students were seen as a **challenge** to the school **authority** — and are more likely to be excluded from school. Gillborn calls this the "myth of the black challenge". Negative labelling could result in a **self-fulfilling prophecy of failure**.

There's also an issue about whether the school curriculum is **ethnocentric** — i.e. that it might fit the mainstream, white, middle class culture better than other ethnicities. It could be **Europe-centred** too. Languages in the National Curriculum are mainly **European** — kids usually learn French and German, not Gujarati or Chinese. **Assemblies**, **school holidays** and even **history lessons** may not fit with the culture and history of particular groups.

Some sociologists see British education as "**institutionally racist**". This is where **policies** and **attitudes** unintentionally discriminate against ethnic minority groups. **Wright (1992)** found that even though members of staff said they were **committed to equal opportunities**, **Asian girls** got **less attention** from teachers and felt their cultural traditions were disapproved of (e.g. they might get told off for wearing a headscarf if it isn't part of the school uniform). **Afro-Caribbean boys** were more likely to be punished and **sent out of class**.

Some sociologists say that these factors may lead to a **low self esteem** for ethnic minorities.
**Coard (1971)** said that black students are made to feel inferior in British schools.

## ***Low Self Esteem*** *Exists — But it* ***Isn't Really All That Widespread***

1) **Mirza (1992)** found that black girls had **positive self-esteem** and **high aspirations**. The girls experienced discrimination but had **strategies** to minimise the effects of racism. It **wasn't low self-esteem** that affected their achievement — it was being **unwilling to ask for help**, or unwilling to **choose certain subjects**.
2) **Mac an Ghaill (1992)** studied 25 Afro-Caribbean and Asian A-level students. He found that all of the students had experienced **some problems** in the education system due to **racism**, but they had generally **succeeded in dealing with these problems** by using different **survival strategies**, e.g. avoiding specific teachers who had a reputation for being racist, while making an effort to build positive relationships with other teachers.

# Ethnicity and Differential Achievement in Education

## Factors Outside School — **Language Difference** Affects Achievement

1) **Language** was a barrier for kids from **Asian** and **Afro-Caribbean immigrant families** when they **first arrived** in the UK.
2) The **Swann Report** found that **language didn't affect progress** for **later generations**.
3) **Driver and Ballard (1981)** also found Asian children whose **first language** was **not English** were **as good at English** as their **class mates** by the age of 16.
4) **Labelling theorists** would say that language might not be a barrier, but **dialects** or having an **accent** might **influence teacher expectations** and lead to **negative labelling**. For example, a teacher might **assume** that a child isn't good at English because they have a foreign accent and put them in lower sets.

## Factors Outside School — **Family Difference** Affects Achievement

1) Some studies say that **family life varies** for different groups and this can influence achievement.
2) **Driver and Ballard (1981)** say that the **close-knit extended families** and **high parental expectations** increase levels of achievement in **Asian communities**.
3) Some sociologists say the high levels of **divorce** and **single-parenthood** in Afro-Caribbean households could result in **material deprivation**. On the other hand, the **independence** of **Afro-Caribbean women** can mean that girls get **positive role models**.

A study at Essex University (2000) found that 39% of British born Afro-Caribbean adults under 60 are married compared to 60% of white adults. 50% of Afro-Caribbean families are single parent families.

## **Ethnicity Combines With Social Class** to Affect Achievement

On their own, the inside school factors and outside of school factors may not seem all that convincing. If you bring **social class** and **material factors** into the equation you get a more complex explanation.

1) The **Swann Report** found that **socio-economic** factors affected the lower levels of achievement of **Afro-Caribbean** pupils.
2) **Pakistani**, **Bangladeshi** and **Afro-Caribbean** groups are more likely to be in **lower class positions** such as routine occupations (assembly line workers, factory workers) and elementary occupations (cleaners, labourers). This may result in poor housing, periods of unemployment, poverty and **material deprivation**.
3) **Chinese**, **African Asian** and **Indian** groups are more likely to be in **higher class** positions and **less likely** to experience material deprivation than other ethnic minority groups.

If you were answering an exam question on this, you'd need to bring stuff from p.50-51 about class and achievement.

## Practice Questions

Q1 Give two facts about ethnicity and educational achievement.

Q2 Why do sociologists disagree with genetic explanations about intelligence and educational success?

Q3 Name one inside of school factor that explains the underachievement of some ethnic minority groups.

Q4 How does language affect educational achievement?

Q5 Give an example of how social class combines with ethnicity to affect achievement.

**Exam Question**

Q1 Assess the significance of inside of school factors in explaining the educational achievement of different ethnic minority groups. (20 marks)

## It's more complicated than you might have thought...

*Remember that not all ethnic minorities underachieve — so don't go storming into your exam answer with a pre-prepared rant that it's all about white / black racism. There are always several different factors that affect each ethnic group. Also, remember that class, ethnicity and gender (see pages 54-55) all mix together to influence how someone does at school.*

# Gender and Differential Achievement in Education

*Gender is another factor that can influence how well people do at school.*
*Since the 1980s, things have changed. Sociologists used to talk about female underachievement.*
*Now there are worries that boys are falling behind. Geez Louise, make your minds up...*

## *Here are **Six Facts** about **Gender** and **Differential Educational Achievement***

1) Girls get **better results** at all levels in National Curriculum tests.
2) Girls get **better results** in **most subjects** at **GCSE**.
3) Girls are **more likely** to **pass** their **A-levels**.
4) Women are more likely to go on to **university**.
5) **Men** seem to have most success at the **highest levels** of University.
   A higher proportion of male students get **first class degrees** and **PhDs**.
6) **Girls** tend to go for **communication based subjects** like English and Sociology and **boys** tend to go for **technical** ones like Maths and Physics.

Don't be tricked by these facts into thinking that boys are doomed.
You could say that there's been a bit of a "**moral panic**" (see page 43) about males underperforming.

## *Understand the **Old Explanations** of **Girls' Underachievement***

There were three explanations for why **girls didn't do as well as boys** before the 1980s:

1) **Biological explanations** said that **girls matured at an earlier age** so they did better at younger ages. Boys would then **catch up** and overtake girls by age 16.
2) Sociologists used **early socialisation** to explain girls' underachievement. They said that **gender stereotyping** started before kids got to school. **Toys** and **media representations** of women helped to socialise girls into the stereotypical roles of **caring** and **mothering**.
3) **Behaviour in the classroom** was also used to explain why boys did better. **Stanworth (1983)** said that classroom interaction **disadvantaged girls**. Girls got **less attention** from teachers and were often **negatively labelled**. **Spender (1983)** argued that education was **controlled** and **dominated** by **men**. The curriculum was **male-centred**, boys got more attention and boys got away with being disruptive in class.

## ***Factors Inside School** Explain Why **Females Now Do Better***

1) **Mitsos and Browne (1998)** say teaching has been **feminised**. Women are **more likely to be classroom teachers**, especially in primary schools. This gives girls **positive role models**.
2) **Textbooks** and **teaching resources** have changed and are less likely to **stereotype girls** into passive roles.
3) The National Curriculum **forced** girls to do **traditionally** "**male**" subjects. For example, more girls started to do **science**. Other Local Education Authority and government initiatives tried to encourage girls to do these subjects, e.g. WISE (Women In Science and Engineering) and GIST (Girls into Science and Technology).
4) **GCSEs** include more **coursework** than earlier qualifications. Some people argue that coursework suit girls better because they put in **more effort**, are **better organised** and can **concentrate** for longer than boys (that's quite a sweeping generalisation though...)

## ***Factors Outside School** Explain Why **Females Now Do Better***

1) Policies such as the **Equal Pay Act** and **Sex Discrimination Act** have helped to create **more equal opportunities** in wider society. This has **changed values** of society and attitudes in school.
2) **Sue Sharpe (1994)** found that girls' priorities have changed. They now want **careers** — and qualifications. More women go out to work, so girls see lots of **positive role models** in work. Girls nowadays often want to be **financially independent** — they don't just want to marry a rich man any more.

The Equal Pay Act (1971) makes it illegal to pay men and women different money for the same work. The Sex Discrimination Act 1975 means employers can't discriminate on the basis of gender.

3) **Boys** tend to spend their leisure time being **physically active**. **Girls** are more likely to spend their leisure time **reading** and **communicating**. This means girls develop **language skills** that are useful for most subjects.
4) The **feminist** movement caused a **change in female expectations**, and made more people **aware of inequality**. People are now more careful about negative stereotyping, sex discrimination and patriarchy.

# Gender and Differential Achievement in Education

## Here are Some *Reasons* Why *Boys Underachieve*

Burly men in Santa hats can read books, too.

1) Boys may be having an **identity crisis**. The rise of **female independence**, the decline of the **breadwinner** role for men and the rise in **male unemployment** might mean that boys don't see the point of education. This may lead to anti-school subcultures.
2) **Interactionists** say that teachers have **lower expectations of boys**. Teacher expectations may lead to a **self-fulfilling prophecy** of poor behaviour. **Negative labelling** may explain why they're more disruptive. Boys are more likely to be **excluded** from school.
3) The **feminisation** of **teaching** means that boys don't have as many **role models** in school.
4) **Reading** is often seen as "uncool" or "girly". Boys who **avoid books** like the plague won't develop important **communication skills**.

## *Subcultures* help to Explain *Gender* and *Achievement*

Negative labelling and putting students into different **streams** or bands can cause some pupils to rebel against school's values. They form **subcultures**. These can be either **pro** or **anti-school** subcultures.

1) In the 1970s **Willis** looked at why working class kids get working class jobs. He studied a group of boys called "Willis's lads". The lads **rejected school** and formed an **anti-school subculture**. They **coped** with their own underachievement by having a **subculture where it didn't matter**, and where having a laugh was more important.
2) **Mac an Ghaill (1994)** says that **subcultures are complicated**. There are **lots of different types**. Boys may join a **macho lad subculture** because of a crisis of masculinity. But boys could also join **pro-school subcultures** and be proud of academic achievement.
3) **Fuller (1980)** found that **Afro-Caribbean girls** in **London** formed a **subculture** that worked hard to prove negative labelling wrong.

## There are *Different Ways to Explain Gender* and *Subject Choice*

Girls tend to go for **arts and humanities**. Boys tend to go for **science and technology**.

1) **Subject choice** may still be influenced by **gender socialisation**. The ideas of **femininity** and **masculinity** create different **expectations** and **stereotypes** of what to study. Kids often see biology as "the science that it's OK for girls to do" and girls who do physics as "super hardcore science chicks" (or "geeky girls who do physics").
2) **Kelly (1987)** found that **science** is seen as a **masculine subject**. Boys dominate the science classroom.
3) **Parental expectations** and **teacher expectations** may encourage girls to follow what they see as the traditional "**normal**" choice for their gender. There's a pressure to **conform** to a social norm.

## *Practice Questions*

Q1 Give two facts about gender and educational achievement.
Q2 Which sociologists studied how classroom interaction disadvantaged girls?
Q3 Name one inside of school factor that explains why girls now do better than boys.
Q4 Who found that girls' priorities have changed?
Q5 Why do subcultures form?
Q6 Give one reason why boys and girls choose different subjects.

**Exam Questions**

Q1 (a) What does the 'feminisation of teaching' mean? (2 marks)
(b) Identify and briefly explain two educational policies that led to improvements in girls' performance. (8 marks)
(c) Assess the significance of factors inside school on the differential progress of boys and girls. (20 marks)

## *Girls are DOOMED... no wait, boys are DOOMED... no wait... ah, forget it...*

*Once again, you can't look at gender without looking at class and ethnicity. Working class girls don't do as well as middle class girls. Also remember that there's a **lot of generalisation** with these sociological theories. Of course not all girls prefer coursework to exams. I bet they prefer lounging around on the beach to doing exams though. Pity they don't test that.*

# State Policy and Education

*All Governments are interested in education. The 1870 Forster Education Act introduced elementary schooling for 5-10 year olds. A few years later all students up to the age of 10 had to do reading, writing and arithmetic. Since then there have been some major changes. Place your votes, please.*

## The 1944 Education Act Introduced the Tripartite System and the 11+

By the time of the Second World War, the main problem was that there was a **huge divide** between the type of secondary education available for the rich and poor. The **1944** Act (often called the **Butler Act** after the man who introduced it) tried to create education for all — secondary schools were made free for all and the school leaving age was raised to 15.
You took the **11+ exam** (like an IQ test) and went to one of three schools:

1) **Grammar schools** were for the able kids who passed the 11+. Pupils were taught traditional subjects ready for **university**. **20% of kids** got in to grammar school.
2) **Secondary modern schools** were for the **75-80%** of pupils **who failed** the 11+. Secondary Moderns offered **basic education**.
3) **Technical schools** provided **vocational** education — hands on **job training** for 5% of the school population.

This **tripartite system** aimed to improve the education of all children, but there remained several problems.

1) The **11+ didn't necessarily measure your intelligence**. It was **culturally biased**, and suited the middle class more than the working class.
2) **Few technical schools were built** so the vocational part of the plan didn't work especially well.
3) The three types of school in the system were meant to have "**parity of esteem**" — **equal value** in other words. The problem was the **grammar schools** were seen as the **best**. Not a surprise, since you had to **fail something** to get into the other two...
4) Kids who failed the 11+ were **labelled as failures** which sometimes turned them off education.
5) If well-off middle class pupils failed, their parents could still afford to send them to **private schools**.

## In 1965 the Labour Government made Schools Comprehensive

The Labour government insisted that Local Education Authorities (LEAs) **reorganised most schools** so that everyone had equality of opportunity. "**Comprehensive school**" means it's universal — everyone's meant to get the same deal.

| **Positive** aspects of the comprehensive system | **Criticisms** of the comprehensive education system |
|---|---|
| There's no 11+, so 75% of the school population don't get labelled as **failures.** | Comprehensive schools still **stream** pupils into sets depending on test scores. (So it's still possible to feel like a failure without the 11+.) |
| **High-ability** pupils generally still do well with this system. Lower ability pupils do better in comprehensive schools than in the old secondary moderns. | Schools in **working class** areas have **lower pass rates** than those in middle class areas. |

The comprehensive system has not achieved equality of opportunity. Schools tend to be "single-class" depending on the local area. Where people can afford to live (and whether there are good schools nearby) is important in educational attainment.

## In 1976 the Push for Vocational Education Started

Labour Prime Minister James Callaghan thought British education and industry was in decline because schools didn't teach people the **skills they needed in work**. All governments since then have had policies to create a closer link between school and work. This is called **vocationalism**.

YTS were job training schemes for 16-17 year old kids leaving school.

1) **Youth Training Schemes (YTS)** started in 1983.
2) In 1993, **GNVQs** and **NVQs** were introduced — **practical qualifications**.
3) The introduction of the **New Deal** in 1997 means people on benefits must attend courses if they don't accept work.
4) Recently, **key skills** qualifications have started. These are supposed to be useful for all jobs.

There are some **problems** with vocational education:

1) Some sociologists argue that vocational education aims to teach **good work discipline**, not skills.
2) Some Marxist sociologists say that vocational training provides **cheap labour** and that governments encourage people into training schemes to **lower unemployment statistics**.
3) Lots of **young people** have **part time jobs** so they **already have work skills**.

# State Policy and Education

## *The* **1988 Education Reform Act** *— Choice, Inspections and More Tests*

In the late 1980s, the **Conservative** government introduced some **major reforms** in education.

### Education should link to the economy

The Government introduced **more vocational courses** and more **work placement schemes**.

### There should be better standards in education

1) The Government introduced a **National Curriculum** of **compulsory subjects** for all **5 to 16 year olds**.
2) **OFSTED** (Office for Standards in Education) was set up to **inspect** schools and make sure they were doing a **decent job**. You might have seen **teachers** getting somewhat **frantic** before an inspection.
3) Schools could **opt out** of their local education authority and become **grant maintained schools**. This means that they got money **straight from the government** and could **spend it how they liked**. The government believed this would **improve standards**.

### There should be a system of choice and competition

1) Parents could **choose** which school to send their child to — if the school had **space**.
2) Parents could use **league tables** to help them choose. **League tables** show **how many** kids at the school **pass their exams**, and how many get **good grades**.
3) Schools worked like **businesses** and **advertised** for students.

### There should be more testing and more exams

Pupils had to sit **SATs** at **7, 11 and 14** and **GCSEs** at **16**.

## **New Labour** *Try To* **Mix** *Some Of The* **Old Ideas Together**

In 1997, New Labour took over. They wanted to do something about **inequality**, but they also said there should be **choice** and **diversity** in education. It's a bit like the old Labour policies and a bit like the Conservative policies, **mixed up together** — it's called "**third way politics**".

The Government has made some changes since 1997:

1) They've **reduced infant class sizes** to a maximum of **30**.
2) They've introduced **numeracy hour** and **literacy hour** in **primary schools**.
3) New Labour have allowed **faith schools** and **specialist status schools**.
4) They've set up **Education Action Zones** to help in areas of deprivation.
5) They've tried to **increase** the **number of people going to university**.

Specialist status schools are schools which specialise in certain subject areas e.g. maths, science or sport.

A big change in 16-18 year olds' education came in 2000. Policy changed to make A-level education broader. Students now have to do **AS/A2s** and **key skills** and there are more **vocational courses**.

The Government are also keen on **citizenship education** to get pupils to be more **aware of politics**.

## *Practice Questions*

Q1 What was the aim of the 1944 Education Act?

Q2 Name the three types of school in the tripartite system.

Q3 Briefly explain two problems with comprehensive schools.

Q4 Briefly describe two changes brought about by the 1988 Education Reform Act.

Q5 Name two changes in schools brought about by New Labour.

**Exam Question**

Q1 Assess the ways in which state policies have influenced educational attainment. (20 marks)

## *Can you ever really solve all the problems in every single school?*

*Governments have been trying to "Sort Out Education Once And For All" and "Shake Up Britain's Failing Schools" for ages. Some education policies have been more successful than others. Whatever happens, kids go to school, teachers teach 'em things, and there's exams at the end of it all — AS-levels, NVQs, vocational A-levels, key skills, GCSEs, International Bac...*

# Poverty and Welfare

*The sociological questions here are: "Which groups have the most / least?", "Is inequality increasing or decreasing?", "How much should the state help the poor?" and "Why does poverty exist at all?" So, that's all pretty straightforward then.*

## Wealth is the Value of a Person's Possessions

Wealth is defined in official statistics as the **value of all the possessions** of an individual **minus** any **debt**. It includes houses, land, money in the bank, shares and personal goods.

Wealth can be divided into **marketable wealth** and **non-marketable wealth**. **Marketable wealth** means **things you can sell**. **Non-marketable wealth** means things like your **salary** or a **pension fund**.

| **Percentage of marketable wealth owned by:** | |
|---|---|
| The richest **1%** of society | **22%** |
| The richest **5%** of society | **42%** |
| The richest **10%** of society | **54%** |
| The richest **25%** of society | **75%** |
| The richest **50%** of society | **94%** |

These figures come from the 2003 edition of Social Trends. The pattern's pretty consistent over the last 25 years, by the way.

1) Every year **government statistics** on **wealth** in the UK are published in the **Social Trends** report.
2) The table shows that **over half** of the country's **wealth** is owned by a **small percentage** of the population. The **less well off 50%** of the population share only **6%** of the country's wealth. These dramatic patterns show a society where **a few people** are **extremely wealthy**.
3) **Wealth** largely results from ownership of **business** and **property**. Most of this gets **passed down** to the **next generation**, so wealth **stays in the same families** for years. However, lots of the richest people in Britain have generated their own wealth (see below).

The *Sunday Times* publishes a list of the **1000 richest individuals** in the UK every year.

1) The 2003 list revealed that the super-rich are **mostly men**. Only 77 out of 1000 were women.
2) 753 of them were **self-made millionaires**, 247 **inherited** their wealth. The ten richest individuals had money from **business** and **land**. The wealthiest individual in Britain in 2003 was the **Duke of Westminster**, but in 2004 it was Roman Abramovich, of oil and football fame.

## Income is the Money a Person Receives on a Monthly / Yearly Basis

1) The vast **majority** of the British population **doesn't have significant wealth**. For most individuals their money comes from an **income**. Income is defined as the **personal funds an individual receives** on a **monthly / yearly basis**. This is usually from a **job** but can be from **benefits**, or **interest** on a savings account.
2) Household **disposable income per head** has **grown steadily** in the UK since the early 1980s. This reflects **overall growth in the economy**, and could be said to show that **everyone is getting richer** to some extent.
3) On the other hand, the **gap** between **rich and poor** has **widened** in recent years (according to Social Trends 2004). This means that the rich are getting richer whilst the poor are getting **relatively** poorer. Ahhh... the stuff sociology is made of...

## There are Patterns of Which Social Groups are likely to Earn the Least

The **Social Trends** report shows how many people have an income of **less than 60% of the median income** (the government measure of poverty). The **median** income is the **middle** income. **Half** the population **earn more** than the median, **half** of them **earn less**.

1) Households where adults are **unemployed** are **most likely** to have an **income below 60%** of the median. Which makes sense — you don't earn a lot of money when you're unemployed.
2) In 2001, **22%** of pensioners lived in households with **incomes of less than 60%** of the median. Which makes sense — you don't earn a lot of money when you're **retired**, either.

The **Social Trends** report also includes statistics about how **ethnicity and income** are related.

1) Overall, people in **ethnic minority households** were **more likely** than people in **white** households to be in the **lowest earning category**.
2) **White, Afro-Caribbean** and **Indian** households were pretty much equally likely to be the **highest earners**.
3) **64% of Pakistani and Bangladeshi households** were in the **lowest earning category**.
4) **White** and **Afro-Caribbean** households were **fairly well spread** across **all income groups**.

# Poverty and Welfare

## *Absolute Poverty* is a Lack of the *Minimum Requirements* for *Survival*

1) An individual is in absolute **poverty** if they don't have the income to afford the basic necessities — **food**, **warmth** and **shelter**. By this definition there are **very few individuals in the UK in poverty**.
2) **Rowntree (1871-1956)** set up the first major studies of poverty in the UK in **1899** and measured it in absolute terms. He made a **list of essentials** needed for life and recorded how many families could **afford** them. Those whose income was **too low** were classed as **in poverty**. He found **33%** of the population in York were in poverty.
3) There are criticisms of Rowntree's study. His definition of poverty didn't allow for any wasted food and it assumed the **cheapest** options were **always available**. The lists of essentials were compiled by **experts** and **didn't match the lifestyle** of the folk he surveyed. He did listen to his critics though, and for two further studies (1941, 1951) he **added more items** to the list of essentials. By this time, **more people** could afford the basics on the list. His conclusion was that **poverty was disappearing fast** in 20th century Britain.
4) Probably the **most recent study of poverty in absolute terms** is **Drewnowski and Scott (1966)**. They devised a "**level of living index**" which worked out the income needed for **basic needs**, adding **cultural needs** to the list. It's debatable whether cultural needs like TV should be included in a study of **absolute** poverty.

## *Relative Poverty* is a *Comparison* with the *Average Standard of Living*

Many sociologists (especially left-leaning ones) favour the **relative** definition of poverty. **Relative poverty** shows whether an individual is rich or poor **in relation to the other people** they **share** their **society** with, rather than whether people have the basics like food and shelter.

### Townsend (1970) studied relative poverty in the UK

**Method** Townsend devised a "**deprivation index**" of 60 items central to social life in the UK. He selected 12 as essential to the whole population — the **level of poverty** was **the percentage** of the population **without** these. Importantly, Townsend didn't just focus on income and material basics but also the ability to have a **normal social life**.

**Conclusion** Townsend's study concluded that in 1969, **22.9%** of the population were living in poverty.

1) Townsend's work has been **criticised** too. **Piachaud (1981, 1987)** said that the deprivation index was inadequate and reflected Townsend's **cultural bias**. **Wedderburn (1974)** thought that the items on the deprivation index were **arbitrary**.
2) **Mack and Lansley (1985, 1992)** did their own research using a deprivation index compiled by **actually surveying the general public** for a list of items essential to social life in Britain. Their conclusion was similar to Townsend — **relative poverty is still a significant problem** in the UK.
3) A **big problem** in measuring poverty like this is that **not everyone agrees** on what the **essential items** are. Sometimes people don't buy something because they **can't afford** it, sometimes they don't buy it because they don't want it.
4) A second problem is that **relative poverty levels** are **constantly changing**, because the economy grows over time. This makes measuring and tackling relative poverty much harder than absolute poverty. **Some sociologists** would argue that this makes it a **less useful concept**.

How much poverty there is out there really depends on how it's **measured**.
With an **absolute** definition of poverty, Rowntree concluded **poverty** was soon to be a **thing of the past**.
With a **relative** definition of poverty, Townsend and others conclude poverty **persists** in the UK.

But then again, it always will because it's relative.

## *Practice Questions*

Q1 Give a one sentence definition of each of the following: wealth, income, relative poverty and absolute poverty.

Q2 How much of marketable wealth is owned by the richest 1% in British society, according to Social Trends, 2003? And how much is owned by the poorest 50%?

Q3 What was Townsend's "deprivation index"?

**Exam Questions**

Q1 Identify and explain two sociologists' definitions of poverty. (8 marks)

Q2 Outline the problems faced by sociologists in defining and measuring poverty. (20 marks)

## We can all dream of being rich...

*Most rows between married couples are about money. It's troublesome stuff, but you can't live without it. Learn the basic pattern of distribution of wealth — if you can learn a couple of figures as well, that'll be useful. Get the difference between relative poverty and absolute poverty sorted — it's crucial for understanding the methodology as well as the theory.*

# Explanations of Wealth Distribution

*Evidence shows that wealth is distributed unequally, and that incomes vary from small to huge. To sociologists, a pattern like this needs explanation — and of course there are lots of different explanations for the way that wealth is shared out.*

## Early Theories **Blamed the Poor** for Being Poor

1) The first theories of poverty **blamed the individual** for the poverty they're in.
2) **19th century** sociologist **Herbert Spencer** said the **poor** were those in society who had **failed** to do the best for themselves. He suggested that they were immoral, lazy and more interested in booze than an honest day's work.
3) Spencer said the **state shouldn't intervene** to help the poor because the poor are a useful **example to others** not to follow that way of life.
4) This attitude isn't necessarily Victorian, you know. The **European Commission Attitudinal Survey 1989** found **18%** of the **British public** thought **laziness** was a cause of poverty.

## **Functionalists** Say **Unequal Distribution** of **Wealth** is **Good** for Society

Functionalism says some people are richer / poorer than others because **society functions that way**. **Functionalist theory** argues that as societies develop, they have to find a way of allocating people to suitable roles and jobs. The most **important jobs** need to be **rewarded more highly than others** to motivate **intelligent people** to **train** and **qualify** for them. The key study to know here is **Davis and Moore *Some Principles of Stratification* (1949)**. Don't worry that it's old – it's classical functionalism.

Functionalist arguments have been **criticised** — they assume the best jobs are allocated on the basis of **talent** when in reality **discrimination** by social class, age, ethnicity and gender often influences who gets top jobs. **Tumin (1967)** reckons that Davis and Moore **ignore all the talent and ability in the working class** which society doesn't use.

## **Weberians** Say Distribution of Wealth is Based on **Market Situation**

1) Weberian sociologists (followers of **Max Weber**) say that the distribution of wealth and income is based on what they call **market situation**.
2) An individual's market situation is how **valuable** their **skills** are for society and how **scarce** their skills are. It's about **supply and demand** of skills. High demand for your skills makes them worth more.
3) For example, currently **plumbers** can earn **higher wages** than other skilled manual workers, because there's a **shortage** of plumbers and people **need their skills**. So plumbers have a good market situation at the moment.
4) Weberians say **poor people** have a **poor market situation**.
5) There **isn't always the same demand** for the **same skills** — the same people don't always have the best market situation. This means there's always some **movement of wealth in society** over time.
6) Individuals **compete** to improve their market situation. **Powerful people** like judges, politicians and the directors of big companies can do most to keep themselves in a good market situation.

Car mechanics are always in demand in the tiger economies.

## **Marxists Blame Capitalism** for Inequalities in Wealth and Income

1) Marxists say that the social groups which have **low levels of wealth** and **income** are the ones which are **powerless** in society.
2) According to Marx and his followers, **capitalism thrives** on **inequality of income** — if there were equal distribution of wealth there wouldn't be any profit for the capitalists. The capitalist class **needs profit** to keep up its **power in society**.
3) Marxism says **exploitation** is an **essential part of capitalism** — and inequalities in wealth and income are a central part of that exploitation.
4) Marx predicted that as capitalism develops, **more oppression** of the proletariat (working class) is needed. Marxists say the current **widening gap between rich and poor** is evidence of this.

As you may have noticed, the Marxist explanations for most things are quite similar. Capitalism, exploitation, etc, etc...

# Explanations of Wealth Distribution

## *Recent **Changes in Society** Have **Increased** the **Gap** between **Rich** and **Poor***

1) The gap between the income of the rich and the income of the poor **went down** in the **1970s**. Under the **Labour government (1974-1979)**, **benefits** given to the poor **went up** and taxes paid by the rich were **very high**.
2) In the **1980s**, under the Conservative government, the **gap widened**. The top rate of tax went down so the **rich kept more of their earnings**. Taxes that everyone pays like **VAT** and **fuel tax** went up. The economy did well so rich people earned more money on their **investments**. **Benefits** went **down**.
3) There has been an **increase** in the number of **single parent households.** Single parent households tend to have less money (see below) and this means the statistics show **more poorer households**.
4) There are also more **two earner households** — e.g. families where both parents work. Income's measured by household, so a **household with two people** in **good jobs** is relatively rich. This contributes to the statistics showing an **increase in rich households**.

## *Some Social Groups are **More Likely to be Poor** than Others*

For these statistics, poverty is defined as having an income that's less than 60% of the average income. Remember that the average income gets pushed up by a few people at the top getting paid huge salaries.

**Women** — in 1992, there were **5.2 million women** living in **poverty** in the UK, compared to **4.2 million men.**
**Older people** — in 1992, **32%** of households where the **main adult was over 60** were poor.
**Single parents** — in 1992, **58%** of **single parents** had an income of less than half the average.
**Disabled people** — in 1996, **47%** of **disabled** people had an income of less than half the average.
**Ethnic minorities** — in 1997, the Policy Studies Institute said that overall UK ethnic minorities are **more likely** to be poor. **Pakistani** and **Bangladeshi** households are the most likely to have **low income.**

1) Women tend to be poorer than men **partly** because they're **more likely** to be **single parents** than men. **Working mums** are more likely to be in **part time jobs** that fit in with childcare — but that pay less.
2) Older people tend to be poorer because they're **retired** — some retired people only get a **basic state pension**.
3) **Single parent** families tend to be poor because it's hard to get **good work** and **look after kids** at the same time.
4) **Disabled** people face **discrimination** in the job market. Disabled people, and people with long-term illnesses who can't work, live on **incapacity benefit** and **disability benefit**, which means they have a fixed, relatively low income.
5) **Some ethnic minorities** tend to be **richer / poorer** than others — and there's **variation** in the level of income within ethnic minority groups. It's not as clear-cut as the statistics suggest.

## *Practice Questions*

Q1 Why did Spencer argue inequality of income is good for society?
Q2 How does an individual's market situation affect their wealth?
Q3 Did the gap between rich and poor decrease or increase in the 1980s?
Q4 Write down five groups in British society who are more likely to be poor than others.

**Exam Questions**

Q1 "Inequality in wealth serves society well". Briefly examine this view from two different sociological perspectives. (20 marks)

Q2 Examine the social composition of the poor in British society. (20 marks)

## *Ever seen how much plumbers charge...*

*Remember that the gap between rich and poor went down, then up again. It's mainly related to tax and benefits. Learn those Functionalist, Weberian and Marxist explanations for distribution of wealth. You can probably guess the Functionalist one "it's all for the best" and the Marxist one "it's cos of evil capitalism, grr". Watch out for those Weberians and their plumber.*

# Why Does Poverty Exist?

*Unsurprisingly, different schools of sociological thought have different explanations of why poverty exists.*

## Oscar Lewis said Culture was the Cause of Poverty

### Lewis (1959, 1961, 1966) studied the poor in Mexico and Puerto Rico

Lewis thought that the **values, norms** and **behaviour** of the **poor** were **different** to the rest of society and these values were passed on to the next generation.

He said individuals learn how to be poor and learn to expect to be poor through the subculture of poverty they're socialised into.

He reckoned that this culture of resignation, apathy and lack of participation in wider society initially starts as a response to poverty but then becomes a culture which keeps people in poverty. He called it a '**design for life**'.

1) Lewis reckoned that the poor are **culturally different** from the rest of society.
2) Lewis's work was **controversial** and **criticised** from the start. Other research done at the same time in similar poor areas found **highly organised community facilities** and **political involvement**.
3) **Schwartz (1975)** concluded that the poor **weren't culturally different** from the well-off.

**Situational Constraints theory** says... guess what it says... it says that the poor are constrained by their situation. I tell you, it's a thrill a minute, this sociology lark.

1) Situational Constraints theory says that the poor have the **same values and norms** as the **rest of society** and any difference in the **behaviour** of the poor is because they're **limited** by their **poverty**. For example, unemployment restricts lifestyle options.
2) **Coates and Silburn (1970)** studied poor areas of Nottingham. They found that **some people** in poor areas **did feel resigned to being poor**, and that it wasn't worth trying to get out of poverty. But... they said this was actually a **realistic assessment** of an individual's situation. It **wasn't proof** of some kind of **alternative value system**.
3) Coates and Silburn's research supported the idea that **poverty leads to other forms of deprivation** which can trap people into a sort of **cycle of deprivation**. This means poverty is **practically hard to get out of**, not culturally hard to get out of.

## New Right Theorists Blame Dependency on Welfare for Poverty

1) **Charles Murray (1993)** described a sector of society which he thought had a **culture of dependency on the state** and an **unwillingness to work**. He called this group the **underclass**.
2) Murray identified three factors — a **rising number** of **single parent families**, **rising crime** and **attitudes** of **resistance to work**. Murray accepts that not all poor people are workshy but he thinks that a significant group of the poor just don't want to work.
3) In Murray's opinion, **Welfare State benefits** are **too high**. He says this means there's not much encouragement to get off welfare and get a job.
4) Another right wing sociologist, **Marsland (1989)** thinks that the **level of poverty** is **exaggerated** by other writers on poverty. He says society should **keep a small level of poverty** to **motivate** others to work. Marsland agrees with Murray that the **Welfare State is too generous** and encourages a **culture of non-work** amongst some groups.

Sociological **criticism** of Murray says his **evidence** for the existence of an underclass is **too weak**. **Walker (1990)** found **very little evidence** of **different values** and **behaviour** among the poor. His opinion was that **blaming** the poor **distracts** from the **real causes** of poverty such as the **failure of social policy**.

## Weberian Sociologists Blame Inequalities in the Labour Market

1) **Max Weber** thought that an individual's **position in the labour market** was the key to their life-chances, wealth and status. The people whose skills were most **valued** and **needed** would always be the **wealthiest**.
2) **Dean and Taylor-Gooby (1992)** think that **changes in the UK labour market** have led to increased poverty. There are more casual and temporary jobs, less job security and there are far fewer "jobs for life". Dean and Taylor-Gooby say this means more people are likely to experience poverty at some point.
3) **Townsend (1970, 1979)** has the view that the key **explanation for poverty** is the **low status** of some workers, which doesn't give them much power to improve their labour market situation.

# Why Does Poverty Exist?

## *Marxists* Blame *The Capitalist System* for Poverty

**Marxists** think that the working class tends to be poor as a result of capitalist exploitation. They say it's a mistake to focus on the poor as a **separate group**, and that poverty comes from **class structure**, so sociologists should focus on the **working class** instead.

Marxists think that **poverty exists** because it **serves the needs of the capitalist class** in society.

You might wonder how poverty can be useful to anyone. Marxist sociologist **Kincaid (1973)** explains it like this:

1) The low-paid provide a **cheap labour supply** for the **capitalist class** which keeps **profits high**.
2) The varying pay levels within the working class keep individuals **competing** against each other to get the best jobs. This **divides the working class**. Remember, the working class is the **majority** in a capitalist society. Marxism says that if the working class all **united together** they'd be a **threat** to capitalism. That's why they say it's in the **interests of capitalism** to keep the **working class divided**.

Kincaid believes poverty is **not an accident** — he thinks it's an **inbuilt part** of the capitalist system. He said, "It is not simply that there are rich and poor. It is rather that some are rich because some are poor."

### Marxists say welfare benefits don't do much good

1) Marxist sociologists **Westergaard and Resler (1976)** argue that state benefits only **blunt the extremes** of poverty.
2) They say that **welfare benefits stay low** to **make sure** that people **still need to sell their labour** even if their wages are low.
3) They also point out that most of the **money paid out in welfare benefits** has been **paid in by the working class in tax** or **subsidised by their low wages.** That means the working class are getting their own money back, not money from the rich. Westergaard and Resler say that the Welfare State "**redistributes within classes** rather than **between them**".

## *Marxist* Explanations of Poverty Have Been *Criticised*

1) Marxist explanations of poverty **don't explain** why some groups in society are much more likely to experience poverty than others. Marxists treat poverty (and just about everything else) as a **characteristic of capitalism**, and as something that the **working class as a whole** suffer. They don't look for much **detail** about the experience of poverty for **individuals** or **groups**.
2) Marxism **ignores** the effects of **gender** and **ethnicity** on poverty. It doesn't explain why women are more likely to be poor than men, or why Bangladeshi households are more likely to be poor than Afro-Caribbean households.
3) **Townsend (1970, 1979) rejects** the argument that the Welfare State doesn't do much good. He believes that **social policy can and should improve standards of living** even within a capitalist system.
4) **Capitalism** creates **wealth** in the economy. This increase in wealth contributes to the **reduction of absolute poverty**.

## *Practice Questions*

Q1 Give an example of an attitude and a behaviour which Lewis (1959, 1961, 1966) argues causes poverty.

Q2 What does Murray (1993) identify as the key processes which create an underclass?

Q3 Give an example of how poverty is helpful to the capitalist class, from a Marxist perspective.

**Exam Questions**

Q1 The claim that the poor are to blame for their poverty features in some sociological explanations of poverty. Critically examine the arguments for and against this view. (20 marks)

Q2 Evaluate the claim that the cause of poverty lies within the structure of society. (20 marks)

## *Blame the victim or blame the system...*

*It's not as easy as you might think to explain why people get stuck in poverty. Each of these theories makes some sense, but they don't all look at the big picture. When you're answering an exam question that asks you to "critically examine the arguments" bear that in mind — remember the downsides of each theory. Use one theory to criticise another.*

# Social Policy and Poverty

*You need to know what kind of things governments do to sort out poverty.*

## The **New Right** believes in the Reduction of the **Welfare State**

1) The **New Right** think that a **generous welfare state** actually **makes people poorer**.
2) British New Right thinker **Marsland (1989)** thinks all **universal benefits** (paid to everyone regardless of wealth) should be abolished because they **encourage dependency**. He says that benefits should only exist to support those in the most desperate need for the shortest possible time. He argues that this will encourage people to "stand on their own two feet".
3) **Right wing policy** encourages **business** so that **wealth will be created**. Right wing politicians would prefer everyone to make their own money and decide how to spend it, instead of paying lots of tax or getting benefits from the State.
4) American sociologist **Murray (1993)** recommended a "**moral**" benefits system to discourage people from forming **single parent families**. He thought that unmarried mums should get no benefit at all.

In the UK, the Conservative governments (1979-1997) were influenced by New Right theory. They **reduced spending** on welfare by removing some universal benefits and having benefits **only for the poorest**. They made it very clear that they wanted to **get rid of the dependency culture** by **reducing benefits** and **allowances**.

The idea was that people would be **better off working**.

The idea was also that resources freed up by these welfare cuts would **boost the economy** which would benefit society as a whole. Conservatives said the money at the top would "**trickle down**" to make **everyone** in society wealthier.

**Examples of Conservative welfare reforms**

1) **Stopped paying benefits** to **16-18** year olds.
2) **Replaced grants** for basic necessities with **loans**.
3) **Abolished** entitlement of **students** to **benefits** in the **academic holiday**.
4) Introduced the **Child Support Agency** — forcing **absent parents** to pay for the support of children, rather than the state.

People on low incomes used to be able to get a "social fund" grant to buy things like a new cooker. Nowadays they can get a loan, which they have to pay back.

So, some of the **New Right solutions to poverty** have **been tried** in the UK. They've been criticised by some sociologists for **increasing** relative poverty.

## **Social Democrats** Believe **Social Policy Reforms** Could Solve Poverty

Social Democrats see **institutions** in society as the cause of poverty. They believe **inequality** in **wealth and income** is the root cause of poverty, so they want government policy to **re-distribute wealth** and resources from **rich** to **poor**.

The big idea is that the state **should** work to stamp out poverty — and that the state **can** work to stamp out poverty.

1) Social democratic theory says **increasing welfare provision** will help to **solve poverty**.
2) **Mack and Lansley (1985)** suggest a big increase in benefits. They conducted a public opinion poll in which British people said they were **prepared to pay higher taxes** to get rid of poverty.
3) **Townsend** sees the solution to poverty in the **labour market**. He says **social policy** must have the job of **reducing inequalities** in the labour market.
4) The poor are most often unemployed or low-paid. This means **policies** are needed to **improve wages** and conditions and to **protect workers' rights**. The **National Minimum Wage** and **Working Families' Tax Credit** brought in under the New Labour government are examples of this kind of intervention.
5) British sociologists **Walker and Walker (1994)** argue for an "active employment strategy" where the government would actually **create work** for the unemployed.

Social democratic theory has been **criticised** by people on the **right wing** and on the **left wing**.

1) **New Right** theorists say the social democratic policy of **strengthening the Welfare State** and increasing the power of social policy would be an **absolute disaster** in terms of solving poverty. The New Right say these things led to the increase in poverty in the first place.
2) Left wing **Marxists** say the **state** will always **serve the interests** of those in **power**, which means that nothing the government does can make a big difference to poverty in capitalist society.

# Social Policy and Poverty

## Since 1997, the **New Labour** Government has had a "**Third Way**" Approach

When New Labour took power in Britain in 1997, it claimed its social policies would reduce poverty significantly. Their philosophy **combines** both the **New Right** and the **social democratic** theories — so it was called "**the third way**".

The theme was that the poor need "**a hand up not a handout**". The "hand up" part means the state should have **social policies** which **help the poor** — rather like the social democratic theory. The "not a handout" part means people **shouldn't depend** on benefits — rather like **New Right theory**.

They say the state has a responsibility to **help people in real need**, and individuals have a **responsibility to help themselves**. The "**New Welfare Contract**" of 1998 says that the **government** has to **help people find work**, make **work pay**, help with **childcare**, help the **poorest** old people and help those who really **can't work**. It says that **individuals** have to look for work, be as **independent as possible**, support their own family, save for retirement and not defraud the taxpayer by claiming benefit when they shouldn't.

Don't worry — you don't need to know all the New Labour social reforms in detail. Here are some examples which help show the ideology behind them.

**Reforms to remove dependency on benefits — so working pays more than benefits...**

1) **Working Families' Tax Credit** — tax reductions for the **low-paid but working**.
2) **National Minimum Wage** — to ensure every employer **pays more than benefit levels**.
3) **New Deal** — a **training** and **support** package for people **returning to work** from benefits.
4) **Welfare to Work** — a series of opportunities for **young, unemployed people** paid for by tax on profits of privatised gas and electricity companies.

**Reforms to make the poor less socially excluded and isolated**

1) **Social Exclusion Unit** — launched to provide support to **re-integrate excluded people** back into society.
2) The concept of **Stake Holders** — individuals could own a stake in organisations which affect them, either in financial terms or voting power.
3) **Child-care costs** paid for or subsidised by the government.

There is conflicting evidence as to whether the government has achieved a reduction in poverty since 1997. The 2003 Social Trends report shows that the distribution of wealth has changed little over the past 28 years. The number of people classed as unemployed has fallen though (see p. 76).

## *Marxists* say *Nothing* Will Work Except the *Overthrow of Capitalism*

1) Marxists believe that the root cause of poverty is the **inequality** central to the **capitalist system**. Therefore, the Marxist solution to poverty is the **removal** of the **capitalist system**.
2) Marxists say that while the capitalist system keeps on going, poverty will still be around — **no matter** what **social policy** you throw at it. **Westergaard and Resler (1976)** think no big **redistribution of wealth** can happen until capitalism is overthrown and replaced by a **socialist** society where **wealth is communally owned**.
3) Marxist theory says that **capitalism** will eventually be **overthrown** — when the working class are sufficiently **united** to have a **revolution**. I wouldn't wait up for it if I were you.
4) The most **common criticism** of the Marxist approach is the **evidence** that **socialist** and **communist societies haven't eradicated poverty**. People were poor in Soviet Russia and there is poverty in Cuba.

## *Practice Questions*

Q1 Why do the New Right think that the Welfare State can be too generous?

Q2 Give an example of a social policy which could be used to reduce poverty.

Q3 Explain how Marxist theory argues poverty could be eradicated in Britain.

**Exam Questions**

Q1 "The New Labour government of 1997 combined opposing policies of previous solutions to poverty in Britain." Explain and evaluate this statement. (20 marks)

Q2 "Ideology lies behind all solutions to poverty." Discuss. (20 marks)

## *Sounds great on paper — but will it work in real life?*

*Although the four theories here are different, they all make some kind of sense on paper. It'd probably be great if everyone earned enough money to buy the best kind of private welfare. It'd probably be great if the state provided really good public welfare for everybody. In real life it's hard to make things work. At the moment, the jury's still out on the Third Way idea.*

# Welfare Provision

*Welfare means all the institutions that look after people — whether they're state-provided or not.*

## ***Four Sectors*** *Provide Welfare —* ***Public, Private, Voluntary*** *and* ***Informal***

### Public Sector

These are **state services** which are **funded, regulated** and **run by the state**. Examples — the **NHS**, the free **education system** and the **benefits system**. Most services are **free at the point of delivery** and are **funded by taxes** and **national insurance**.

### Private Sector

These services are **run by companies for profit**. They often offer **alternatives** to state services — e.g. **private hospitals, schools** and **nurseries**. There's no state funding but they have to **meet state regulations**. The individual **pays for these services directly**.

### Voluntary Sector

These services are provided by **charity**. They often provide **extra** facilities and services beyond what the state provides. E.g. the **hospice** movement and **Help the Aged**. They have to **conform to state regulations**. Voluntary services **may get some state funding**. The individual receives these services **free** or at a **subsidised low cost**.

### Informal Sector

This means services and help provided by **friends and family** as and when needed. The informal sector often provides services **in addition to state services** or when there **isn't enough state provision**. Examples — **family carers, family childminders**. There's **little** or **no state funding** or **regulation**. It's usually **free** to the individual but **costs the provider money**.

In the British system **all four sectors are mixed together**. The **Conservative** governments of 1979-1997 encouraged more **private** and **voluntary** sector welfare provision and less **public welfare provision**. The New Labour governments since 1997 have not attempted to change this substantially.

## ***The Welfare State*** *—* ***Health, Housing, Education, Social Work*** *and* ***Benefits***

1) The British **Welfare State** was set up in the **1940s** after the **Beveridge Report** was published. The Welfare State was designed to wipe out the social problems of society. Beveridge defined these as the "**five evils**".

- **Ignorance** (poor education) → **1944 Education Act**
- **Disease** (poor health) → **NHS set up in 1946**
- **Want** (poverty) → **National Insurance Act**
- **Idleness** (unemployment) → **National Assistance Act**
- **Squalor** (poor housing) → **Council Housing Programme**

2) People in work would pay into a **national insurance scheme** which would **pay for the Welfare State**. The Welfare State was designed to be free at the point where you actually needed it. For example, going to the doctor = free.

3) The British Welfare State is **universal**. This means all benefits and services are given to **everyone** rather than **selectively** to the poorest. **Checking** that people are **poor enough** to get a selective benefit is called **means testing**.

4) The **cost of the Welfare State** has **risen a lot**. The Office of National Statistics said 61% of the total government budget was spent on welfare in 1993.

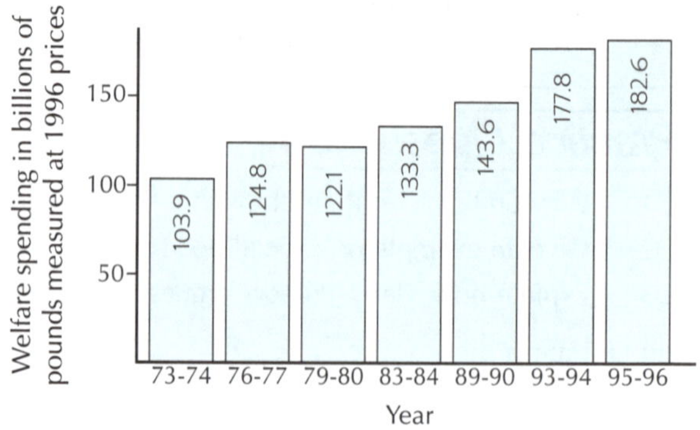


There have been a lot of **Conservative reforms** to **reduce the size** of the Welfare State and **cut costs**.

1) **Increase** in **selective benefits** — e.g. 1980 Housing Act, 1988 Social Security Act.
2) **Reduction** in **universal benefits** — e.g. general entitlement to free eye tests abolished.
3) **Privatisation** of welfare provision — e.g. local authority care homes closed, replaced by private care homes.
4) **Increase** in **voluntary** and **charitable** welfare provision — e.g. housing associations taking over council houses.

Under **New Labour** there's been an emphasis on trying to make the NHS and social security more **efficient** to **save money**. Most benefits and services cut by the Conservative governments **haven't been re-introduced**.

# Welfare Provision

## *Social Democrats believe the Welfare State can Reduce Inequality*

The founders of the Welfare State thought it'd **reduce inequality** because the rich and poor would all get the **same benefits** and **services**. Resources would be shared out more **equally**. Part of the vision of the Welfare State was that these policies would help create a society where all people had **equal opportunities**. But...

...There's research demonstrating **persistent hard-to-shift inequality** in all five areas of welfare — **health**, **education**, **housing**, **unemployment** and **poverty**. A good overall study by **Le Grand (1982)** found not much evidence of redistribution of resources. Le Grand found that **middle class** families were more likely to use the free services of the welfare state — not the working class, or the poor.

**Marxist** sociologists **Westergaard and Resler (1976)** argue that the welfare state has failed to reduce inequality between social classes in Britain. Their research focused on **tax** and **benefits**, and concluded that the **working class contributed most** as a **proportion** of their **income** and that the **middle class benefited the most**. However, the middle classes as a group pay most in terms of the total tax received by the government. Some sociologists have argued that by focusing on the contribution as a proportion of total income, **Westergaard and Resler** emphasised the inequality aspect.

## *The New Right Prefer Selective Benefits and Means-Testing*

1) Remember, the New Right theory blames poverty on an **over-generous welfare state**.
2) So, from the New Right point of view, the ideal welfare state has a **small range** of **minimal benefits** which are only selectively available to the very **poorest**.
3) Selective benefits would be **means-tested** — the government would only provide them to people whose incomes were below a certain level.
4) The New Right say that governments must focus on creating a **strong economy**. In a strong economy **private welfare providers** can compete giving individuals **choice** and **value**. New Right thinkers reckon the **free market economy** is the **best way** to ensure services are provided at the **lowest prices** and the **best quality**.
5) The New Right think that a **strong market** will encourage individual endeavour, leading to an increase in standards of living for everybody. The Welfare State would only be needed as an **emergency back-up**.

## *For Marxists the Welfare State Reproduces and Legitimises Capitalism*

1) According to Marxists, the Welfare State makes sure the capitalist class always has a **healthy workforce** through the NHS. For Marxists, they don't do this to be **nice** to the individual worker but to **keep them working**, which is essential to keep **making profits**.
2) The Welfare State helps to portray the image of a **caring society** where the state **cares** for the individual. Marxists say this is **useful** to the capitalist class because it **hides** the real **oppressive** nature of capitalism and **keeps the working class quiet** — which prevents a revolution.
3) Not all Marxists agree, mind you. An **alternative Marxist view** is that the **Welfare State exists** because it was **fought for** by **workers' struggle** and the capitalist class wouldn't have provided it otherwise.

## *Practice Questions*

Q1 Name four sectors which provide welfare.

Q2 What were the key social problems the Welfare State was founded to address?

Q3 List four Conservative reforms of welfare provision.

Q4 Outline the findings of Le Grand (1982).

**Exam Questions**

Q1 "The Welfare State has successfully reduced inequality in British society". Evaluate this statement. (20 marks)

Q2 Compare and contrast Marxist and New Right theories of the Welfare state. (20 marks)

## *Shall we give the poor some money, or shall we not bother...*

*You might think that the New Right theorists are all mean old grumpyboots with no heart, or that Marxists are just dreamers with no grip on reality. The thing is, they both genuinely believe they're doing the best for everyone. With these social policies, it's hard to tell who's wrong and who's right. You can look at real-life examples — most of these ideas have been tried somewhere.*

# Management and Organisation of Work

*What's work for one person might be leisure for another. If I play golf it's leisure (and better golfers might say it's also comedy). When Tiger Woods plays golf it's work. Luckily, sociologists agree on some characteristics of what constitutes work.*

## Ideas about Work and Leisure are Fairly Modern

You **get paid** for work.

Work is **not primarily** done for **pleasure**.

At work there is an **employer** or **boss** who's **in charge**.

There's a **clear distinction** between **time at work** and **leisure time**.

There's a **wage contract** which sets out **what kind of work** is exchanged for **how much money**.

The **distinction between work and leisure** is a **modern** idea. Before the Industrial Revolution, things were **less clear cut**. **Capitalism** and **industrialism** are the two big forces influencing work and leisure in the modern age.

## Capitalism and Industrialism are Defined in Terms of Work

### Capitalism is commodity production

Marx defined capitalism as "**commodity production**". A **commodity** is a **product** made **for sale**, **to make profit**. **Modern capitalism** involves these three features.

1) There's **private ownership** of the **means of production** (means of producing wealth).
2) **Labour power** (work) is **purchased** by employers for **wages** — work therefore becomes a "**commodity**".
3) The **overriding driving force** in capitalism is to make lots of lovely, lovely **PROFITS**.

### Industrialism is mechanised commodity production in factories

Industrialism is the **mechanised production** of commodities by workers in **industrial plants** and **factories**. The production process is **managed** and **coordinated** by **specialist managers**.

## Mechanised Assembly Line Production was Introduced in the 20th Century

In 1911 **Frederick Taylor** devised a system of management called "**scientific management**". He used **time and motion studies** to see what workers spent their time on. He developed the idea of a **division of labour** — recommending that work should be broken down into smaller and smaller **specialised tasks** to increase control and profitability. Henry Ford put the idea into practice with his assembly line for making cars.

**Henry Ford** had the very first **moving assembly line** in the **Ford car factory** in 1914.

1) **Fordism** is a term for **industrial assembly line production**.
2) Assembly lines produce a **standardised product** that the **mass market** can afford.
3) Work is divided up into lots of **little repetitive tasks** which are done by a **line of workers** along a **moving conveyor belt or track**. The conveyor belt **carries the product** from one worker to the next, and **each worker does their bit**. Each worker does the **same thing** over and over again **all day**.
4) Workers **don't need to be skilled** to work on an assembly line. Most are unskilled or semi-skilled.

## Braverman Claims Labour is Progressively Deskilled under Capitalism

1) **Harry Braverman (1974)** said that under industrial capitalism work is **degraded**. Workers become **deskilled** — their jobs used to need skill, but don't any more. **Fordism** leaves workers with boring, repetitive jobs, and almost no say in how they do their jobs. Braverman said this would get **worse and worse** as technology and mechanisation progressed.
2) Braverman bases a lot of his ideas on Marx's concept of "**alienated labour**". Marx believed that under capitalism work is **alienated** from the worker by capitalism's **obsession with profits**. There's **loads** more on this on page 71.
3) Braverman has been criticised for **exaggeration**. Some sociologists claim that workers are often **compensated** for their lack of control over the labour process through **good wages**.

# Management and Organisation of Work

## *Post-Fordism* is *Flexible* and Involves *Multi-Skilled Labour*

Remember — **Fordism** means **repetitive, deskilled assembly line work** that keeps **costs low**.

Braverman suggested that **Fordism** will **intensify** as **technology advances**. Several sociologists **disagree** and say there is a new "**post-Fordist era**" in the management and organisation of work.

### Main Features of Post-Fordism

1) **Computer technology** — technological development means that **many of the boring repetitive** tasks of the factory can be done by **computer controlled machines**.
2) **Skilled labour** — modern firms require more **flexible** and **versatile, multi-skilled** workers rather than **unskilled** production line workers.
3) **Flatter Management** — there's **less strict hierarchy**. Modern firms involve workers in **decision-making**. This means the workers are more **committed** to the firm.
4) **New Organisation of Workers** — British economist **John Atkinson (1986)** reckons that the new industry organises its labour force in terms of **core workers** and **peripheral workers**. Core workers are **multi-skilled and motivated**. They're **full time employees** of large companies and tend to be disproportionately **white** and **male**. Peripheral workers are **low paid, temporary contract workers**. Peripheral workers are disproportionately **black** and **female**.
5) **Products Made for Quality not Quantity** — Products are aimed at a **discerning niche market**. It isn't mass production for a mass market any more.

## *Neo-Fordism* is a *New Kind of Capitalism*

Some sociologists say that **post-Fordism** isn't really a good thing. They say it's more like **neo-Fordism** — a new kind of Fordism in slightly different clothes.

1) **Paul Thompson (1989)** thinks that rather than requiring **skilled flexible workers** modern firms simply train workers to **multi-task**, so that they can perform **any simple repetitive** task on a production line.
2) **Marxist sociologists** also say that **mass production isn't on the decline** — it's simply upped and moved to countries where the labour is cheaper. This is called the **globalisation of mass production**.
3) **Anna Pollert (1988)** thinks that the **peripheral** work force **isn't a new development** for capitalism at all. She says it matches with the desire to **maximise profits** by **reducing costs**. The use of a peripheral, temporary work force has made it simple to **weaken** the **trade unions** and **reduce industrial conflict**. Pollert calls this "**coercive pacification**" — making it so workers can't make a fuss.

Quick and Easy Profits No. 5.
Switch your factory to gold production.

## *Practice Questions*

Q1 Give five features of work (as opposed to leisure).

Q2 What is meant by industrialism and capitalism?

Q3 What is meant by scientific management and Fordism?

Q4 What is deskilling?

Q5 What are the main features of post-Fordism and neo-Fordism?

**Exam Question**

Q1 Assess the validity of the post-Fordist views on the organisation and management of work. (20 marks)

## *Everything we do — is driven by a need to increase the profit margin...*

*You need to know the definitions of capitalism and industrialism before you start. A lot of the theory of management stuff is about factory work where workers make things on an assembly line. Make sure you learn the list of features of post-Fordism. Of course, you wouldn't expect all sociologists to agree on anything, so there's points to learn against post-Fordism as well.*

# Work: Satisfaction, Alienation and Conflict

*The next four pages are about explanations and theories relating to attitudes to work.*
*I suppose you've probably got a fairly decent attitude to work if you're reading this book. Go you.*

## Many People think that **Today's Society** has a **Positive Attitude** to Work

According to sociologist **Keith Grint (1991)** this wasn't always the case in past societies.

1) In **prehistoric, hunter gatherer societies** it's unlikely there was any work ethic at all. Once enough food had been found then work stopped completely.
2) In **classical societies** like Ancient Greece and Rome, work was often rather **looked down on** and usually associated with slaves.
3) **Before** the **Industrial Revolution**, most people **worked at home** and were paid for each bit of work they completed. Workers had a degree of **control** over the work process. Evidence suggests that domestic workers saw work as a **necessary evil** and **resisted all attempts** to make them **work harder**.

Grint's work suggests that work has only become important to people in the modern industrial era. Wonder why that is...?

## **Max Weber** Suggests the **Protestants** Gave Society its **Work Ethic**

**Calvinism** is a **strict** kind of **Protestant Christianity**.
It emphasises work and says **work** is a **calling from God**.

**Max Weber (1958)** identified **Calvinism** as an **important influence** on the **work ethic** of society today. **Victorian** attitudes to work were quite Calvinist. Victorians saw work as a **moral duty**, and they were very **harsh on laziness**.

Others, for instance social historian **E.P. Thompson (1967)**, have suggested that the **Industrial Revolution** was behind the development of the modern work ethic. The Industrial Revolution introduced **working in factories** which demanded a change in attitudes towards work.

There was a big change from **task orientation**, where you work until a task is finished, to **time orientation**, where you keep working for a set time. If you worked at **home**, you could **stop for a break** any time you liked, but **machinery in factories** had to **keep going** through the **whole day**. At the start of the Industrial Revolution, workers had to be **taught** by employers to **work hard all day long** and not **waste time**.

## **Functionalists**, **Marxists** and **Feminists** have **Different Ideas** About Work

### Functionalists

Functionalists like **Emile Durkheim** take a **positive** attitude to work in industrial society. Durkheim compared the **different work tasks** carried out in a **modern economy** to the **different functions** carried out by the **different parts of the body**. Each function is needed for society or the body to **function harmoniously**. Durkheim referred to this as **organic solidarity**.

### Marxists

Marxists see work in capitalist economies as characterised by **exploitation**. The big idea of Marxism is that a **small minority own the means of production** — the raw materials and machinery used to make things. Workers **create wealth** by working, but they only get a **tiny bit of it back** as wages. Marx also believed that under capitalism labour is **alienated**. There's a lot more about the alienation of labour on the next two pages.

### Feminists

Feminists argue that there's a **sexual division of labour** which **excludes women** from **important** areas of work and restricts them to **low status areas**. Traditionally, there were "men's jobs" and "women's jobs", but this is changing. Up until the late 20th century, women (especially middle class women) were **discouraged** from **working outside the home** at all. Feminists point out that **most domestic labour** is done by women, and that nobody gets paid a penny for doing **housework**.

# Work: Satisfaction, Alienation and Conflict

## Marx Believed a **Person's Ability to Work** was Really Important

Marx said the **ability to work** was a person's **most important attribute**. It's **through work** that people can **change** and **improve** their world.

He thought that under **capitalism** labour gets **alienated** from this positive role and instead turns into a series of **boring**, **repetitive**, **uncreative** tasks.

## **Alienated Labour** is More than Just Boredom at Work

According to Marx, labour is **alienated** in the following ways:

1) Labour becomes just another **commodity** that can be bought and sold. Labour is alienated from its true role — it **doesn't belong to the workers** any more and they can't do what they want with it.
2) Workers' **tasks** under industrial capitalism are **boring**, **repetitive**, **uncreative** and **highly controlled**.
3) The **worker** becomes **powerless** because the capitalists own both the **labour process** and the **products** of labour. In Marx's language, the capitalists own the **means of production** and the **products of labour**.
4) The profits from a worker's labour are made to **work against the worker** by being **invested** back into the **capitalist system**.
5) Workers are also **alienated from each other** under capitalism because it's a **competitive** system.

## **Marxists** say Workers' Labour is **Alienated** — Even if They **Don't Realise It**

For a Marxist, alienation is "an objective state due to the social relations of production". This means it's something that **definitely** happens to **all workers** because of the way **capitalism** is organised. Process workers and assembly line workers are **exploited** and their **labour is alienated** — **whether they feel it and believe it or not**. Marxism says that workers will only be free from alienation under **communism**.

**Wright Mills (1951)** found that it isn't only **manual workers** who suffer alienation. **Office workers** and **sales people** are alienated because they have to put on a **mask** of being "**nice**" or "**sincere**" and **can't express** their **real attitudes**.

## **Functionalists** are **Optimistic** About Industrialisation

1) **Durkheim** (writing in the 1890s) disagreed with Marx, and was fairly optimistic about industrialised labour. Durkheim suggested that **specialisation** could eventually **increase social cohesion** as people became **more dependent** on each other and therefore more likely to work together.
2) But Durkheim was **concerned** that the **rapid speed of industrialisation** would lead to a state of "**anomie**". Anomie literally means **normlessness** — it means a state of confusion where **nobody knows how to behave**. The **upheaval** of industrialisation would be so huge that people **wouldn't share the same norms** and **values**.
3) Durkheim said **rising divorce rates** and **industrial unrest** were **evidence of anomie**. In some ways it was a similar idea to Marx's idea of alienation.
4) **Marx** thought that the only solution was to **overthrow the system**. **Durkheim** thought the solution was **codes of practice** between workers, owners and professionals to make the **existing system nice and workable**.

## Practice Questions

Q1 Who said the work ethic in modern society came from the early Protestants?

Q2 Give three examples of ways that Marx said work could be alienated from the worker.

Q3 What is meant by organic solidarity?

**Exam Questions**

Q1 (a) To what extent is the work ethic a modern phenomenon? (20 marks)
(b) Discuss Marx's theory of alienated labour under capitalism. (20 marks)

## Well, paint me green and put me on Mars...

*Marx said that your labour is alienated even if you say it isn't. So, even if you like your job, Marx would say your boss is exploiting you by making you do boring work and keeping the profits from what you do. Thompson makes pre-industrial life sound nice — stopping for breaks any time you liked, being as lazy as a very lazy person from Lazyville. Was it really like that, though..?*

# Work: Satisfaction, Alienation and Conflict

*Here's more on alienation from work and workers' attitudes to work...*

## *Blauner Says* ***Alienation of Labour*** *Has* ***Four Sources***

1) **Powerlessness** — When workers **aren't in control** of their work process or activity.
2) **Meaninglessness** — When workers **don't see** the **function** or **meaning** of their activity in the context of the whole organization. Labour is alienated if you **don't know why** you're doing what you're doing.
3) **Isolation** — When workers **don't** see themselves as part of a **social group** or **community** in the workplace.
4) **Self-estrangement** — When workers **don't get involved** in their work and don't use it to express themselves.

### Blauner (1964) Studied Workers' Attitudes

**Method:** Blauner gave **questionnaires** to workers in different industries — a traditional print shop, a textile mill, a car factory with a production line and an automated chemical plant.

**Findings:** From his results, Blauner figured that **different industries** have **different levels of alienation**. He found little alienation in craft technology (traditional printing) and a lot of alienation in assembly line production (the car factory). Blauner found very **little alienation** in **fully automated production**, because the boring manual work is done by industrial robots. Blauner thought that workers in automated production have plenty of responsibility and control — they operate a control panel to make sure the machines are doing the right thing.

**Conclusion:** Blauner thought that **production technology** was a big influence on alienation. He saw **automated production** with computerised industrial robots as the way forward.

Automated factories have computer-controlled machines. The machines do the production line work instead of human workers.

Marxists criticise Blauner, saying he **ignores the real causes** of alienation. Others criticise Blauner because they think he **interpreted** what workers said in the questionnaires in a **biased** and **unscientific** way.

## *Some Workers* ***Don't Mind Alienation*** *— They're* ***Happy*** *with the* ***Money***

### Goldthorpe et al. (1969) studied process workers

**Method:** They surveyed a sample of 229 manual workers and 54 white-collar workers to find out about their **attitudes to work**.

**Findings:** They found that many manual workers **didn't** actually **expect job satisfaction**. They were prepared to put up with being bored and frustrated in return for **relatively high wages**. Goldthorpe et al. called this an **instrumental attitude** towards work — work as a means to an end. Good pay allowed workers to have a nice lifestyle and give their families a good standard of living.

**Conclusion:** Goldthorpe et al. concluded that many workers actually chose "alienating work" because it paid better. These "**affluent workers**" didn't look for satisfaction in their work. They looked for satisfaction and enjoyment in their **family life**.

You can say there's two types of job satisfaction. Intrinsic job satisfaction is pleasure workers get from work itself. Extrinsic job satisfaction is when workers enjoy good wages — and get satisfaction from what they can buy with them.

**Some sociologists** have **criticised** Goldthorpe et al. for **two main reasons**:

1) The men they studied weren't representative. They were all **married with kids** and perhaps more likely to be "instrumentally orientated" — concentrating on supporting their family. The men surveyed were **earning significantly more than the national average** — not all assembly line-type jobs do pay well. Also, they didn't study any women.
2) **Neo-Marxists** have suggested that the **preoccupation with lifestyle** and **what you can buy** is the result of exposure to a **capitalist mass media**.

## *Neo-Marxists Say* ***False Needs*** *Hide Alienation*

The neo-Marxist **Herbert Marcuse (1964)** said that **work is horrible**, and **leisure time isn't much better**.

He said that **leisure** activities are mainly based around what he calls **false needs** — things people **don't really need**, and which **don't really satisfy** them. False needs are fed to workers through the **mass media**. Marcuse gives cars, expensive hi-fi equipment, fancy homes and expensive kitchen equipment as examples of false needs.

Marcuse calls workers who go after these false needs "**happy robots**". He says that **fulfilling a false need** results in a "**euphoria in unhappiness**" — a temporary high which hides the misery of alienation.

Marcuse suggests the term "**happy consciousness**" as a new version of traditional Marxist "false class consciousness". This "happy consciousness" gives people the **false impression** that **leisure makes them happy**.

# Work: Satisfaction, Alienation and Conflict

## *Industrial Action* Means *Conflict* Between Workers and their *Bosses*

There are **different types of industrial action**:

1) **Strike** — This is when workers **collectively withdraw their labour** — in other words, **stop working**. Strikes are often organised by trade unions.
2) **Sabotage or theft** — When workers **deliberately damage or steal equipment** belonging to the company they work for.
3) **Work to rule** — When workers only work to the **letter** of their contracts and won't do any tasks that aren't on the contract.
4) **Absenteeism** — When workers **deliberately go absent from work** without good reason.

A trade union is an organisation of workers usually centred round a particular trade that collectively negotiates on behalf of all its members — e.g. National Union of Mineworkers, National Union of Teachers.

## There are *Many Different Reasons* and *Theories* as to *Why Strikes Start*

1) **Boredom** and **resentment** makes strikes more likely. In a study of strikes in the textile industries, **Edwards and Scullion (1982)** concluded that most strikes were caused by boredom and resentment of bad management.
2) **Communications failure** makes strikes more likely. Workers who find it hard to express grievances are more likely to go on strike.
3) **Wage disputes** account for over 40% of strikes in Britain. However in a study of the Pilkington glass workers, **Lane and Roberts (1971)** concluded that strikes that were **supposedly about wages** were often **really about worker resentment of management**.
4) **Certain groups of workers** seem to be **more likely** to go on **strike**. **Kerr and Siegel (1954)** concluded that **dockers** and **miners** were more likely to strike because they were **geographically and socially isolated**. This meant they tended to have a strong sense of solidarity with each other. This is called **isolated mass theory**.
5) **Marxists** see strikes as **inevitable byproducts** of an **exploitative capitalist system**. Marxists are often lukewarm about trade unions — they think collective bargaining legitimises the capitalist system.
6) **Agitators** sometimes cause strikes. An agitator is someone who gets **other workers** all worked up and **angry** about a situation and makes them **more likely to strike**.

## *Industrial Action* is On The *Decline*

If you read the papers you might think people are **on strike all the time**. In fact, the number of strikes has been **going down** significantly since the **1980s**. Sociologists suggest the following reasons:

1) **Trade union laws** made it more **difficult** to call strikes. Some forms of industrial action have been made **illegal**.
2) **Trade union membership** has **fallen** a lot since the 1970s and 1980s.
3) **High unemployment** in the 1980s meant that workers became **less willing to risk their jobs** by striking.
4) **New Right** sociologists argue that increasing affluence means fewer people feel the need to strike.

## Practice Questions

Q1 What are Blauner's 4 elements of alienation at work?

Q2 Give two criticisms of the work of Goldthorpe et al. (1969).

Q3 Give three reasons why workers might go on strike.

**Exam Questions**

Q1 Suggest three factors which may affect the degree of job satisfaction experienced by workers. Briefly explain your choices. (6 marks)

Q2 "The function of leisure is to distract workers from their true alienation at work." Discuss. (20 marks)

## Show me the money...

*It's hard to answer a question like "Are workers satisfied at work?" because it really depends on the particular worker, their boss and the company they work for. Sometimes people don't mind doing a tedious job if it pays well. Sometimes people fall out with their bosses and go on strike. Back in the 1970s, striking was pretty common, but it doesn't happen as often now.*

# Impact of Technology

*These pages will help you revise the impact of technology on the experience of work.*

## Sociologists Disagree about Technology

### Technological Determinists See Technology as a Force Which Affects People

Technological determinists think technology is an **independent force** which forces work to be organised in a particular way. A good example of a **technological determinist** is **Blauner** (see page 72), who identified a link between technology and job satisfaction / alienation.

### Social Determinists Think People are in Control of Technology

Social determinists think people control technological change. **Social forces** determine how technology develops and people **make choices** about how they're going to **react** to it. **Goldthorpe et al.** are good examples of **social determinists** — they claimed that workers' **attitudes to work** affected how they reacted to technology.

## Here are Views from Three Contemporary Sociologists

### 1) Shoshana Zuboff is in between Social and Technological Determinism

**Shoshana Zuboff (1988)** claims that "**smart machines**" are having a **really important impact** on the workplace — but **human choices** will decide whether it's a **positive** or **negative** impact. Zuboff says that with ICT (information and communication technology), managers can choose to **automate** the workforce — cutting jobs, controlling work and deskilling. Or they can "**informate**" the workforce — adding value to jobs, giving workers more control, reskilling.

Hmmm, "informate"... sociologists do tend to make up odd words like this.

### 2) Jon Clark adopted a position closer to a technological determinist one

**Clark, McLoughin, Rose and King (1988)** studied the adoption of new computer technology in **British telephone exchanges**. They concluded that once a new technology is set up and running, it gets very difficult for workers to change their relationship to the new technology. Clark identified **critical junctures** (**moments**) during the introduction of technology when people can **influence** the way technology is used. However **once these moments had passed**, workers were **stuck** with the way they were using the technology. In Clark's words, "**social chances** became **frozen** within a given technology".

### 3) Rob Kling believes that the impact of computer technology depends on how it's used

**Rob Kling (1991)** rejected both Zuboff and Clark's conclusions about the impact of computer technology on work and **rejects any deterministic theory** that claims computers will **definitely** have a particular effect on work. According to Kling computers can **deskill** but they can also **reskill**. Sometimes computers have a really big impact and sometimes they have virtually **no impact** at all. It all depends on how they're used or **consumed**.

Technology can be **consumed in different ways** leading to very **different results**. For instance — if A-level students are given **fixed times** to use **computer suites** their lives become **regimented** by when they can use them. However, if they had **open access** to the technology to use it in their **own time**, the **effect of the technology** on **how they work** would be quite **different** — although the **technology itself is identical**.

## Here's a Summary of their Positions

| | |
|---|---|
| **Zuboff** | There's been a **computer revolution** — this can have either a **positive** or a **negative** impact on the experience of work. **Managers** can **choose** what the impact will be. |
| **Clark et al.** | Once computer technology has been put into place, it can **limit** and **freeze** someone's work **opportunities** and **experiences.** |
| **Kling** | The effect of computer technology on the experience of work mainly depends on how it's **used** or **consumed.** |

# Impact of Technology

## The **Way People Talk About Technology** May **Influence** How it's Used

1) **Keith Grint and Steve Woolgar (1992)** studied how people **talk** about technology.
2) Grint and Woolgar **attack** the idea that **technology determines the effect it has** on the workplace **by itself**. They say it's **impossible** to **separate** a technology from the **interpretation** that people put on it — what people think about it in other words.
3) They argue that the **way people talk about technology** is the **crucial factor** in how technology will be applied in society. The people who succeed in **spreading their view about technology** are in a **powerful position** to use technology in their own interests. They point out that power isn't equally shared in the discussion about technology — recognised **experts** have a **disproportionate** amount of power.

Ethel and Rita's discourse on technology was going swimmingly.

Grint and Woolgar's work is interesting because it shows there are always **choices** about how a technology is used. But they can be **criticised** for **exaggerating** the influence that individuals have over how technology is used.

The talk about technology is called "the discourse surrounding it" in sociologists' language. Grint and Woolgar also refer to people as "social actors". Again, it's just the way sociologists are.

## **New Technology** and **Manufacturing Techniques** Can Lead to **Exploitation**

1) **Harry Braverman (1974)** did a **Marxist** critique of mass production. The "**Braverman Thesis**" (also known as the "**deskilling thesis**") says that mechanisation leaves workers with low pay and unfulfilling work, because work gets **deskilled**. **Relations** between **bosses** and **workers** get **worse**. Braverman thought that this process would get faster as technology developed.

2) **Andrew Zimbalist (1979)** did a case study of the American **printing** industry which described the **deskilling** of labour by technology. Years ago, printing was a very **skilled** job. Every single letter on the page was put into place by a **skilled worker**. Zimbalist says that the **deskilling** of the printing industry led to the **print unions losing their power**.

3) **Andy Friedmann (1977)** is more **critical** of the Braverman thesis, suggesting that other factors may well be important. He is also more hopeful about the potential for **workers to influence** the **application of technology** — some workers would get more control over their own work.

4) **Shoshana Zuboff (1988)** found that some **office workers** felt that their jobs were becoming **deskilled**. She said that **automation** meant that jobs which used to have **face-to-face skills** were now done in front of a **machine**. Workers felt that they were forced to sit in front of their computer with their **heads down**, and **weren't allowed to talk** to each other. However, she also found that computer technology could also be used to **help communication** between workers, e.g. email.

## Practice Questions

Q1 Who claimed that attitude and orientation affected how people reacted to technology?

Q2 Who claimed that managers can choose to either "automate or informate" the workforce? What does this mean?

Q3 Give an example of how the way that a particular technology is consumed can have different effects on the workforce.

**Exam Questions**

Q1 Sociologists disagree about the impact of technology. Explain two important sociological theories about this issue, with reference to the individual sociologists that support them. (20 marks)

Q2 Critically assess the Braverman Thesis, with reference to ideas from other sociologists. (20 marks)

## *Let's talk about fax, baybee...*

*Does technology rule people or do people rule technology...? Unsurprisingly, sociologists tend to think it's somewhere in between. Technology does change things, but people have the chance to influence how they use technology. At the end of the day though, if your boss comes in and says, "Here's a new computer system, use it!" then you're gonna be using it.*

# The Social Effects of Unemployment

*Sociologists argue about the causes and consequences of unemployment.*
*In fact, they can't even bring themselves to agree about how it should be measured...*

## *Unemployment in the UK Goes Up and Down*

1) **Structural unemployment** is where a whole **big bunch of workers** lose their jobs because their **skills aren't needed** any more, e.g. when coal mines close.
2) **Cyclical unemployment** is where people lose their jobs because the **economy** is on a **downer**. When the **economy perks up** again, more **jobs are created** and unemployment goes down.
3) **Frictional unemployment** is where people lose a job and quickly get another one.

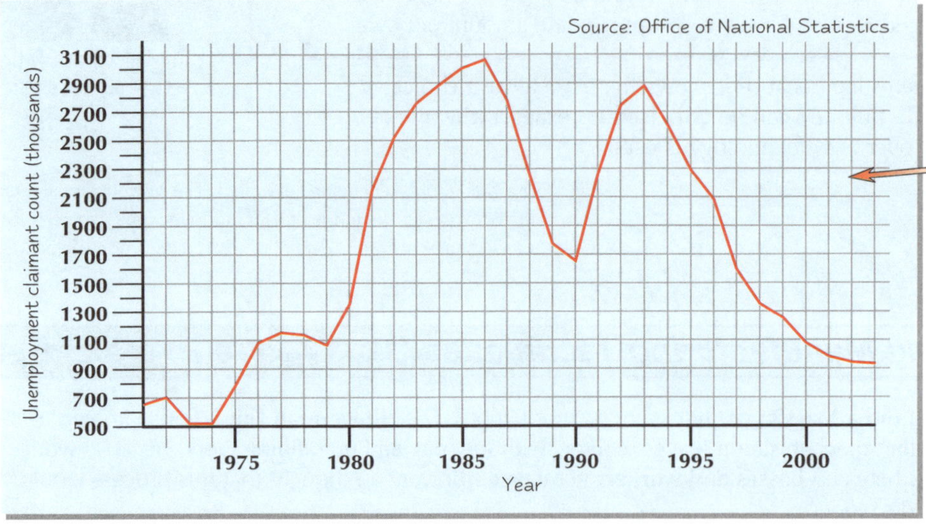


You can also look at the number of people claiming unemployment benefit as a percentage of the population. This went from 1.9% in 1973 to 10.5% in 1986, then down to 5.5% in 1990, back up to 9.7% in 1993 and down to 3.1% in 2003. You can also make an estimate of how many people are unemployed but not claiming benefit.

## *It's Hard To Measure — Some say the Figures are Fiddled*

**Measuring unemployment** isn't as easy as you might think:

1) **Not everyone** who's out of work **registers** for **Jobseekers' Allowance**.
2) People who **have to leave work** because they're **ill** or **injured** **sometimes count** as unemployed and sometimes not.
3) **Housewives don't count** as unemployed — or employed either.
4) People who take **early retirement** sometimes count and sometimes they don't.

The problem of benefit fraud could be said to be a moral panic (see p. 43).

Politicians tend to suggest that **official unemployment figures** are **overestimated** because they include people who actually work but still claim Jobseekers' Allowance — "**benefit fraudsters**". There's not much hard research evidence to back up this position. **Pahl (1984)** found that the unemployed were no more likely to do informal cash-in-hand work than the employed.

The **Trade Union Congress** (TUC) suggest that unemployment is actually **underestimated** by around 1.5 million. Governments keep **changing the method** of calculating unemployment. The TUC think that governments change it to **get a lower figure each time**, so it'll **look like** unemployment is **going down** faster than it really is.

## *Not All Social Groups face the Same Risk of Unemployment*

1) **Older workers** are more likely to be made **redundant**. **Young people** don't have the **experience** needed for many jobs. You could say both groups are victims of **ageism** in society.
2) **70% of the unemployed** are **unskilled manual workers**. The lower a person's skill level, the more likely they are to be unemployed.
3) **Ethnic minority groups** generally have **more unemployment** than the white population. This is partly down to **discrimination** and partly down to **differential levels of achievement in education** (see section 5).
4) There are big **regional** differences in unemployment in the UK. Unemployment hot spots include the **North**, **North West**, **Northern Ireland** and **Wales**, where there's been a **decline of traditional heavy industry** like steel works and mining. Unemployment is a lot **lower** in the **South East**, where there's been a big increase in the number of **service sector jobs**.

# The Social Effects of Unemployment

## Sociologists give Conflicting Causes for Unemployment

1) **Keynesian views — it's demand**
Followers of economist **J.M. Keynes** think unemployment is caused by **low demand** in the economy. Keynesians believe **state policy** and **investment** can raise **demand**.

2) **Marxist views — it's capitalism**
Capitalism benefits from **some unemployment** because a "**reserve army of labour**" keeps wages down. Even if **you** don't want to work for **low wages**, some **unemployed** guy probably will.

**UNEMPLOYMENT**

3) **New Right views — it's tax and welfare**
The New Right viewpoint is that **high business tax rates** hurt business and cause unemployment. They also think **welfare benefits** mean some people **don't bother to get a job**.

4) **The global economy — jobs are going abroad**
Some sociologists argue that unemployment is due to the **manufacturing** industry **moving** to countries like China, the Philippines and Vietnam. Such moves benefit businesses because **labour costs less** and there are **fewer regulations**.

## There's Less Disagreement on the Negative Effects of Unemployment

No one in Sociology says, "Well, unemployment's not that bad really, you get to watch daytime TV".

1) **Poverty** — **Income** from benefits is **low**. When there's not much money coming in, **standard of living** is **low**. **Housing problems** start because it's hard to pay the **rent** or **mortgage** (although people on low incomes can get housing benefit). It's often difficult to get new rented accommodation if you don't have a job.
2) **Social effects** — **Stress** and **no money** often cause **family arguments** — and more **stress**. Unemployed people often feel **isolated** from the world of work and they're **socially isolated** from other people.
3) **Physical health effects** — Unemployed people tend to have **worse health** than working people. There's more **long term illness** and disease among people who have been unemployed for a while.
4) **Mental health effects** — Unemployed people are more likely to be **clinically depressed** — it's not surprising that being unemployed is **depressing**. A person's sense of **identity** is often closely linked to their job. So if they **lose** that job, they lose that part of their identity, and as a result can feel **insecure** or **purposeless**. Unemployed people have **higher rates of suicide**.

Long-term unemployment can lead to a **dangerous spiral downwards** — the unemployed person becomes **less and less able** to **rejoin the world of work** as their self-esteem, mental health and physical health all go into decline. This can affect **whole communities** — e.g. some mining communities were badly affected after the pits closed.

## Practice Questions

Q1 What are structural, cyclical and frictional unemployment?
Q2 Why is it difficult to trust official statistics on unemployment?
Q3 Give four possible causes of unemployment.
Q4 Give four consequences of unemployment for individuals.

**Exam Question**

Q1 Discuss and evaluate different sociological viewpoints on the causes of unemployment. (20 marks)

## Gizza job, go on, give us one, I know you got one...

*Unemployment is a total bummer. That much is agreed. Different sociological theories have different ideas about why unemployment happens, though. An interesting thing about unemployment is how hard it is to measure — two sets of figures from different years might have been measured in completely different ways, which means you can't really compare them.*

# Leisure

*Some people think it's quite easy to distinguish leisure from work — leisure's the time "left over" after work. It's not so clear cut for everyone, though. So, what do those sociologists make of it all...*

## Parker Defined Categories of "Life Space"

**Stanley Parker (1976)** came up with these definitions of different ways people spend their time:

| | |
|---|---|
| **Work** | Time spent in paid employment |
| **Work obligations** | Time spent as a result of paid employment, e.g. commuting to work |
| **Non work obligations** | Time spent on activities such as child care or housework |
| **Physiological obligations** | Time spent eating, sleeping, washing, and on the loo |
| **Leisure** | The time left over. |

## Parker Says the Type of Work you do Shapes your Attitude to Leisure

1) **Professionals** who have plenty of **independence** and **job satisfaction** show an **Extension Pattern** of work and leisure. The boundary line between work and leisure isn't always clear because **work is a central part** of that person's **life**. Leisure activities are often linked to work activities, for example a businessman might meet clients on a golf course.
2) **Clerical** and **semi-skilled workers** with less independence and job satisfaction show a **Neutrality Pattern** of work and leisure. There's a clear divide between leisure and work. Work isn't so important to the person. **Family life** and **leisure** are the central interests in life.
3) **Unskilled manual workers** working **tough** and **dangerous** jobs have an **Oppositional Pattern** of work and leisure. There is a **very clear distinction** between work and leisure. Leisure is of **central** importance and is used to "**compensate**" for hard work. Leisure activities are **fun**, not serious.

Stanley Parker has been **criticised** for **ignoring other sociological factors** which may influence attitudes to work and leisure, such as gender, culture and class.

## Marxists say Leisure is Shaped by the Nature of Capitalism

Marxists claim that **before the industrial revolution** and the rise of capitalism there was **no clear dividing line** between work and leisure. The introduction of the **factory** system meant workers had to **work longer hours** in more **structured** surroundings. "Leisure time" as such only began to **emerge** in the **late 19th century**. The **freedom** and **flexibility** that people had before industrialisation **never** returned.

1) Under **capitalism**, leisure has been **commodified** and **commercialised**. It now involves the passive consumption of "leisure commodities" by consumers — things like films, going to the pub, going to bingo, going out to a restaurant. According to neo-Marxists **John Clarke and Chas Critcher (1985)**, the two most important influences on leisure are the **state** and the **leisure industry**.
2) The **state regulates leisure activities** through licensing of pubs, bars, clubs and gambling. It regulates films and TV by censorship. This means that leisure opportunities are limited.
3) Marxists say that "bourgeois" middle class pursuits like playing golf and going to restaurants are seen as more **worthwhile** than working class ones like going to the pub.
4) The **leisure industry** is big business making huge profits. **Commercialised leisure** is **dominated** by **large companies** who, Marxists say, **manipulate choices** and **tastes** and **exploit** consumers.

## Pluralists see the Leisure Industry as a Democratic Market Place

**Ken Roberts (1978)** sees leisure as a **freedom of choice** thing. He **rejects** the Marxist idea that leisure is defined and imposed on consumers by big business and government. Roberts takes a **democratic pluralist** view of the leisure market place, where state and commercial providers have to **respond to public tastes**. If the leisure industry didn't give people what they wanted, they'd **lose money**. Roberts says that leisure must involve **freedom of choice** — if you had to do it, it wouldn't be leisure.

# Leisure

## **Feminists** Say **Men's Experience** of **Leisure** is Different to **Women's**

1) Feminists point out that men and women do **different leisure activities**.
2) Women have **less access to leisure** because of relatively **low incomes**, **discrimination** in society and **stereotypical views** on women's domestic responsibilities.
3) Women who go out to work often have to do the **housework** as well. They have **less time available for leisure** than men.
4) **Looking after children** is **stereotypically women's work**, and women do most childcare in the UK. Childcare responsibilities don't leave much time for leisure. Also, looking after children is sometimes characterised as "spending all day playing with them".

**Liberal feminists** seek a **reformist** solution to these problems. They want to highlight discriminatory practices and get them reformed. Liberal feminism would like **equal pay**, access to free or **subsidised childcare**, and an **end to discrimination**.

**Radical and socialist feminists** suggest that gender inequality is created by the **patriarchical structure** of society and that only wholesale change in that structure will change women's experience of work and leisure.

## **Postmodernists** Claim that **Individuals Choose** their Leisure

**Traditional sociology** says that class, gender, age and ethnicity have **some bearing** on **everything** we do. **Postmodernists** say that the effects of class, gender, age and ethnicity are on the **decline**.

1) Postmodernists such as **Lash and Urry (1993)** have claimed that advances in satellite, cable and Internet technology and the globalisation of culture has made leisure more **individualised** or "**privatised**".
2) **Consumers** have an absolutely **huge** number of **leisure choices** in postmodern society. Leisure activities are used by consumers to construct "**unique social identities**" for themselves. These unique identities aren't tied to gender, ethnicity or class.
3) Lash and Urry also suggest that people are **less likely** to take part in **group** leisure activities than they were in the past.

Critics of the postmodernists point out the lasting influence of **class**, **gender** and **ethnicity**.

For instance **ethnic minority consumers**, living in inner cities with low level incomes and suffering the negative effects of **racism**, are unlikely to have access to 'postmodern' leisure activities. But on the other hand, it's different for well-off ethnic minority consumers living in the suburbs.

Feminists such as **Scraton (1994)** point out that women's **leisure opportunities** are **still** largely shaped by a relative lack of **disposable income**, societal expectations of **gender roles** and "open ended domestic responsibilities".

## Practice Questions

Q1 How does Stanley Parker (1976) distinguish between work and leisure?

Q2 What is meant by:

a) an Extension Pattern of work and leisure;

b) a Neutrality Pattern of work and leisure;

c) an Oppositional Pattern of work and leisure?

Q3 In what ways do men and women experience leisure differently?

**Exam Question**

Q1 Suggest three reasons why the leisure patterns of the unemployed might differ from the leisure patterns of the employed. (6 marks)

## A bit of time off — now there's a good idea...

*Leisure is a big part of modern life — and it's big business. Because it's big business, you can be sure that Marxists will have something snarky to say about it. You can argue that media and big business manipulate people's leisure interests and push people into liking films and football and pubs and bingo. On the other hand, you could say people just enjoy those things.*

# Key Issues in Research and Methods

*Sociologists do research to get evidence which helps them understand society. Unfortunately, it's not all that straightforward to study human behaviour. If only we were ants in an ant farm.*

## Sociologists Have Three Aims When Collecting and Using Data

1) Sociologists try to make their research **valid** and **reliable**. Research is **valid** when it gives a **true picture** of what's being measured. Research is **reliable** if other sociologists using the **same methods** get the **same data**.
2) You can't research the whole population. You have to take a **sample** (see page 82). Sociologists try to make sure that their **sample represents the population** — it needs similar proportions of different ages, gender, class and ethnic groups.
3) Sociologists aim to be **objective** and **avoid bias**.

If a study focuses on a particular group, e.g. teenagers or working class people, researchers must still ensure that their sample is representative of that particular group.

**Sociologists get data from different sources**

1) **Primary sources of data** involve **first hand research** — things like interviews, focus groups, questionnaires or observations (see p. 90).
2) **Secondary** data includes things like **official statistics**.

**Data can be either quantitative or qualitative**

1) **Quantitative data** is **numbers** and **statistics**. You can easily put quantitative data into a graph or a chart.
2) **Qualitative** data gives a detailed picture of what people do, think and feel. It's **subjective** — it involves **opinions, meanings** and **interpretations**. You can't turn qualitative data into a list of numbers or a graph.

## Positivists Use Reliable Methods That Give Quantitative Data

1) **Positivists** say behaviour is influenced by **external social factors**.
2) They think sociology should be **scientific** and **analyse social facts**. Social facts are things that **affect behaviour** and can be **easily measured**. They're **external** things like laws, **not internal** things like people's opinions.
3) Positivists look for **cause and effect relationships**. They investigate questions like, "Does poverty **cause** underachievement in schools?"
4) They use methods like **questionnaires** and **official statistics**. These are **objective** and **reliable**. They produce **quantitative** data.

## Interactionists Use Valid Methods That Give Qualitative Data

1) **Interactionists** (also called **Interpretivists**) use methods that let them discover the **meanings**, **motives** and **reasons** behind **human behaviour** and **social interaction**.
2) Interactionists reckon that the **scientific** methods used in **positivist** research **don't tell you much** about how **individual people** act in society.
3) Interactionists say you can't count meanings and opinions and turn them into statistical charts. They reckon **sociology isn't scientific** because **humans can't be measured** like ants in an ant farm. People don't always understand questions in questionnaires and they don't always tell the truth to researchers.
4) Interactionists like to use methods that produce **qualitative** data — they try to understand human behaviour from the point of view of the **individual person**. They use methods like **participant observation** and **unstructured interviews** that give a valid and detailed picture of what individual people think.
5) **Max Weber** said it's important to use **empathy** to **get inside a person's head** to figure out **why** they're doing what they're doing. He called this "**verstehen**" ('understanding'). Interactionists take this idea of Weber's very seriously — they're big on empathy.

Participant observation means being actively involved in the research as both participant and observer.

**Positivism** looks at the **institutions** in society. It's called **macro sociology**.
**Interactionism** looks at the **individual**. It's called **micro sociology**.

# Key Issues in Research and Methods

## Theoretical Background Affects your Choice of Method

| Theoretical background | Positivism | Interactionism |
|---|---|---|
| Explanation of behaviour | It's determined by **social forces beyond people's control**. | Humans actively **make sense** of **social situations** during human interaction. |
| Aims of sociology | Sociology should discover **what causes what.** | It should **describe** and **explain** how people **make sense** of situations — using **empathy**. |
| Research methods | **Questionnaires** and **structured interviews** — they give **quantitative data** and they're **reliable** and **objective.** | **Observations** and **unstructured interviews** — they give **qualitative data** and a more **valid insight** into society. |

## Ethical Factors Affect your Choice of Method

The **British Sociological Association** gives **ethical guidelines** for research. Researchers should use **informed consent** — people should know who's doing the research, why they're doing it and what it's about. **Covert participant observation**, where people don't know a sociologist is watching them, should only be used when there's **absolutely no other way** of obtaining data.

Researchers studying **sensitive issues** like domestic violence often choose to use **informal interviews** to put the person answering the questions **at ease**.

## Practical Factors Affect your Choice of Method

1) **Time** — Some methods need more time. **Covert participant observation** takes a **long time**. The researcher has to get into the group they're studying and win their trust before starting the actual research. A **social survey** doesn't need the researcher to participate all the time and the **workload can be shared** in a team.
2) **Money** — This affects the **length** and **method** of the research. Money is needed to **pay the researcher(s)**, for **transportation** to interviews and to pay for **resources** like computers. **Large scale social surveys** are **expensive**. The 1991 Census cost £135 million. A small focus group will cost a lot less.
3) **Characteristics and skills of the researcher** — It'd be difficult for a **female** researcher to be involved in a participant observation of **monks** in a monastery. Some researchers may be OK with **dangerous situations** and others may prefer to **stay at their desk** and do **detailed analysis** of statistics.
4) **Access and opportunity** — If researchers **don't have access** to certain groups to carry out interviews or observations, they have to turn to **secondary sources**. Sometimes researchers don't get the **opportunity** to get data from certain people, e.g. they might be too **busy** to fill in a questionnaire.

## Practice Questions

Q1 Why do sociologists carry out social research?

Q2 What is the difference between quantitative and qualitative data?

Q3 Name two characteristics of positivism.

Q4 What type of data do interactionists prefer?

Q5 Briefly explain how practical factors affect your choice of method.

**Exam Questions**

Q1 (a) What is meant by the term validity? (2 marks)

(b) Identify three criticisms positivists would make of interactionists. (6 marks)

(c) Examine the different factors that influence the sociologist's choice of research method. (20 marks)

## Ready, aim, research...

*Sociologists use different methods to produce different types of data. Positivists and interactionists prefer different research methods. There are also ethical and practical factors which influence which method you choose. Remember that funding is a huge factor — sociologists don't work for nowt, y'know.*

# Surveys

*Sociologists choose to use different research methods when they carry out social research. Some methods produce quantitative data. Others produce qualitative data. There are lots of different methods and lots of different problems.*

## Before You Can Start — You Need a Sample

1) It's **too expensive** and **time consuming** for sociologists to involve the **whole population** in their research. They select a **sample**. Only the census includes everyone.
2) When they select the sample they usually try to make it **represent the population** under study — with similar proportions of people in terms of age, class, ethnicity and gender.
3) If the population is **homogenous** (all the same) the sample needs to be homogenous. If the population is **heterogeneous** (all different), the sample needs to be heterogeneous.
4) **Random sampling** is where names are selected at random from a list of names called a **sampling frame** e.g. a class register in a school. Random sampling is often more representative than non-random sampling.

**How to do random sampling**

1) **Simple random sample** — Pick names **randomly** from a list. Everyone has an **equal chance** of being selected.
2) **Stratified sample** — Divide the population into groups and make a **random selection** with the **right proportions** (if 60% of the population is male, 60% of the sample must be male).

**How to do non-random sampling**

1) **Snowball sample** — Find an **initial contact** and get them to **give you more names** for your research.
2) **Quota sample** — Pick people who fit into a certain **category** (e.g. 15 people between 30 and 40).

## A Pilot Study Lets You Have a Practice Run

1) A pilot study is a **small-scale** piece of research used as a **practice run**. You might want to **test** the **accuracy** of your **questions**, or **check** to see if there are any **technical problems** in your research design. You do this to make the study **more valid** and **more reliable**.
2) You can also **test how long** the research will take, **train** your **interviewers** and get **research funding** — once you show your project is useful.
3) Pilot studies are **time-consuming** and **expensive** and they create a **lot of work**.

## Social Surveys Give Quantitative Data

1) **Social surveys** collect information about a large population, using **standardised questionnaires** or **structured interviews**.
2) Social surveys tend to be used by **positivists** as a **primary source** of **quantitative data**.
3) Standard questionnaires and structured interviews are **reliable**. They're used by **government agencies** and **research companies**.

Townsend used a 39 page questionnaire in his 1979 research on poverty.

## Longitudinal Studies are Social Surveys Over a Period of Time

**Longitudinal studies** are done at **regular intervals** over a **long period of time**. They're often **large scale quantitative** surveys, and they tend to be used by **positivists**. Some TV programmes like *Seven Up* are more **qualitative**.

*Seven Up* was a TV documentary that asked 14 kids aged 7 what they thought about life, and what they wanted to be when they grew up. The programme makers came back to interview the children every seven years. The latest instalment was *Forty-Two Up*.

**Strengths of longitudinal studies**

1) You can **analyse changes** and **make comparisons** over time.
2) You can study how the **attitudes** of the sample **change** with time.

**Limitations of longitudinal studies**

1) It's **hard** to recruit a **committed sample** who'll want to **stay** with the study.
2) It's **hard to keep contact** with the sample, which may make the study less valid.
3) You need **long-term funding** and you need to **keep the research team together**.
4) Longitudinal studies rely on **interviews** and **questionnaires** which might not be **valid** or **reliable**.

# Surveys

## *Questionnaires* Mainly Give *Quantitative Data*

**Questionnaires** mainly use **closed questions** and standardised **multiple choice answers** — e.g. "What's your favourite fish? Tick *cod, haddock, salmon, sea bass, tuna* or *other*". Don't forget though that some questionnaires use **open-ended** questions.

Questionnaires mainly give you **quantitative** data which positivists like. **Standardised questions** make them **reliable**. A questionnaire with **open-ended questions** can give you some insight into **meanings** and **motives**. They give you **qualitative** data. The **reliability** and **validity** of a questionnaire depends on **how it's designed**.

**Questionnaires should...**

1) Use **clear, simple questions** which are **easy to understand**.
2) Give **clear instructions** and make it **easy** for the respondent.
3) Have a nice **clear layout** that doesn't **intimidate** people.
4) Give a **range of options** on **multiple choice** questions.
5) **Measure** what **you want to measure**.

*The person answering the questionnaire is called the respondent.*

**Questionnaires shouldn't...**

1) Ask **embarrassing, threatening** or **complex** questions.
2) Ask **two questions instead of one**.
3) Be **too long**.
4) Use **sociological** terms that **no one understands**.
5) **Lead** the respondent to **answer a question** in a **particular way**.

*Blauner used questionnaires in his (1964) study of workers' attitudes in different industries* (see p. 72).

**Strengths of questionnaires**

1) They're **quick, cheap** and they can reach lots of respondents.
2) They're **reliable** because the questions are **standardised**.
3) They're **easy to analyse** with computer programmes.
4) There's **no interviewer** to **affect** people's answers.
5) You can **spot patterns** in the answers and **make comparisons**.

**Limitations of questionnaires**

1) Respondents **may not tell the truth**.
2) Questions may be **misleading** or **mean different things** to **different people**. They may not measure what you actually **want** them to measure.
3) Postal questionnaires have a **low response rate**. If it's **too low** it won't be a **representative** sample.
4) **Open ended questions** make it **hard to quantify the data** into nice neat **numbers**.
5) No one can **explain** the questions if the respondent doesn't understand them.

## *Practice Questions*

Q1 Why do sociologists select a sample?

Q2 Briefly explain two types of sampling methods.

Q3 What are the benefits of carrying out a pilot study?

Q4 What is a social survey?

Q5 What type of data do questionnaires mainly produce?

Q6 Name two problems with questionnaires.

**Exam Questions**

Q1 (a) What is meant by a longitudinal study? (2 marks)
(b) Identify three problems with longitudinal studies. (6 marks)
(c) Assess the usefulness of questionnaires in sociological research. (20 marks)

## *I had to give a sample at the doctor's, don't say I need one here as well...*

*Pick your sample first, then do a pilot study. Check what you're doing is really as valid and reliable as you'd like it to be. Questionnaires are harder to work out than you might think — you've got to give sensible options for multiple choice questions, and you've got to make the questions really clear and easy to understand.*

# Interviews and Observations

*These pages are about getting primary data from interviews and observation.*

## *An **Interview** is a **Conversation** Between a **Researcher** and a **Respondent***

1) An **interview** is a **conversation** between a **researcher** and an **interviewee** where the researcher asks a set of questions.
2) You have to pick the **sample**, organise an **interview**, select / train your **interviewers**, **ask the questions** and **record the answers**. **Bias** can get in the way in each step. An interviewer should create a **friendly, relaxed atmosphere**.
3) An **interviewer effect** is when the **response** given isn't what the interviewee **really thinks**. This can be caused by the **gender**, **age**, **class** or **personality** of the interviewer. The **opinions** of the **researcher** and **interviewer** can **influence** the interviewee.

## *Structured Interviews = Quantitative Data, Unstructured ones = Qualitative Data*

1) **Structured interviews** ask the **same standardised questions** each time. The questions are closed questions, with set **multiple choice answers**.
2) They give **quantitative data** and they're very **reliable**.
3) They're used in **large-scale social surveys**.
4) The interviewer can **explain** and **clarify** the questions.
5) Structured interviews can ask the **same questions** as a questionnaire, but they get a much **higher response rate**. People tend to agree to be interviewed.
6) They're **more expensive** than questionnaires — you need to **pay for the interviewer**.
7) The interviewer has to **follow the list of questions** so they **can't ask for more detail** if the respondent says something **particularly interesting**.

Edgell used interviews in his (1980) study of decision making by middle class couples (see p. 21).

1) **Unstructured interviews** are **informal**, with **no rigid structure**.
2) They're good for researching **sensitive issues** where the interviewer has to gain the respondent's **trust** — for example sexuality, domestic violence, crime.
3) They use **open ended questions** and give **qualitative** data. They're quite **valid**.
4) The interviewer needs to have **skill** so they can **probe** to **find out more detail** about the interviewee's **beliefs** and **opinions**.
5) They're used with **smaller samples**, which means they're **not very representative**.
6) There are a lot of **interviewer effects** in an unstructured interview. The interviewee may say what they **think** the **researcher wants to hear**.
7) It takes a **long time** to write up an **unstructured interview** — you have to write down a **whole conversation**, not just the **codes** for particular **multiple choice answers**.

## ***Ethnography** Studies the **Way of Life** of a Group*

1) **Ethnography** was first used by **anthropologists** to study **traditional societies**. They joined the community, learnt the language and noted their observations.

Anthropology is the study of humans.

2) It's small-scale field work that tends to produce **qualitative** data. It's **valid** because you can study behaviour in **natural settings**.
3) You can use all sorts of methods to get **ethnographic data**. You can use **unstructured interviews**. You can **observe** a community and see what they get up to.
4) **Case studies** are in-depth studies of **particular events** like **demonstrations**.
5) You can find out an **individual's life history** with **interviews** and **observations**.
6) **Time budgeting** is where you ask people to keep a **detailed diary** of their activities during a specified time. This can create **qualitative** and **quantitative** data.
7) Researchers may also analyse **diaries** and **letters**, which are **secondary data**.

- Ethnography is **in-depth research** which gives **inside knowledge** about a community.
- You get a **valid** picture from ethnography, but it relies on the **researcher's interpretations** of what people do and say.
- It's **difficult** to **make generalisations** from small-scale research.

# Interviews and Observations

## Observation is Watching Behaviour in Real-Life Settings

1) In **covert observation**, the researcher **doesn't tell the group** they're being observed. The BSA advise that you should only use covert participant observation when there's **no other way** of obtaining the data. For example, **Nigel Fielding (1993)** used covert observation when researching the National Front (a far right-wing political party) because he believed he would encounter hostility if they knew he was a sociologist.
2) **Overt observation** (direct observation) is when the group is aware of the research and they know who the researcher is. For example, **Beverley Skeggs (1991)** used overt observation when studying female sexuality among students at a college.
3) **Participant observation** is when the researcher **actively involves themselves in the group**.
4) **Non-participant observation** is when the researcher **observes** the group but isn't actively part of the group.

Interactionists prefer observation because the researcher can get to the action. It tends to produce qualitative data that's more valid than questionnaires.

## Participant and Non-Participant Observation Have Pros and Cons

### Participant observation

1) Participant observation gets the researcher **right to where the action** is — so they can **check out the dynamics of a group** from **close up**.
2) **Participant observation** allows you to research the workings of deviant groups.
3) The researcher gets a **first hand insight** of people in **natural real life settings**.
4) If it's **covert**, people **can't mislead** the researcher.

**But...**

1) The researcher may get too involved and find it **hard to stand back** and **objectively observe** the group.
2) You **can't repeat the research**. It **lacks reliability**. A covert observer may find it difficult to remember all the events and accurately record them.
3) There are **ethical** and **practical** problems in **getting in**, **staying in** and **getting out** of the group.
4) **Overt research** may **influence** the behaviour of the group.
5) The researcher in a **covert observation** may join in with illegal acts if they're in a deviant group.
6) The research usually involves a **small group** so it's not **representative** of the population.
7) It's **hard work**, **time-consuming** and **expensive**.

### Non-participant observation

1) In **non-participant** observation, the researcher **isn't drawn into the group** so they can be more **objective** about the group's behaviour.
2) If you want to observe **deviant** groups, you have to be very **inconspicuous**.

**But...**

1) **Observing from the outside** stops you from getting to where the **action** is.
2) **Overt research** may **influence** the **behaviour** of the group.

## Practice Questions

Q1 Give two differences between structured and unstructured interviews.

Q2 What is ethnography?

Q3 Which research methods could you use to carry out ethnographic research?

Q4 What is the difference between covert and overt observation?

Q5 Briefly explain two strengths of participant observation.

**Exam Question**

Q1 Assess the usefulness of unstructured interviews to sociologists. (20 marks)

## Sociologists could be everywhere, watching us... shhhh...

*It's annoying, this tendency people have to say what they think the researcher wants to hear. Can you really trust anything someone says in an interview...? I dunno. Participant observation gives access to people, but it's difficult to do and you won't necessarily get the same results twice. I don't think I'd want to do a participant observation of serial killers.*

# Experiments

*You can use experiments to give you quantitative primary data.*
*You can get quantitative secondary data from statistics, and qualitative secondary data from documents.*

## *Experiments Let You Find Cause and Effect*

Testing a hypothesis with an experiment is called the Hypothetico-deductive model.

1) Experiments are used by **natural scientists** — biologists, chemists etc.
2) The researcher starts with a **hypothesis** and they use the experiment to **test** it out.
3) All the variables are kept constant, apart from the one you're interested in — the **independent variable**. Scientists **change the independent variable** and observe the effects on the **dependent variable**. If you were testing the effects of temperature on electrical resistance, **temperature** would be the **independent variable** which **you control** and **electrical resistance** would be the **dependent variable** which you **measure**.
4) The results are **turned into numbers** — the scientist looks for **patterns** and **cause and effect** relationships.
5) This method has been developed and used by **social scientists** to look for **social** causes and effects.

## *There are Three Kinds of Experiment*

1) **Lab experiments** are done in a **controlled environment**. The researcher **changes** the **independent variable**. The researcher observes the effect on the **dependent variable**. The researcher generally uses a **control group**, which is **left alone** to see what happens if you **don't do anything** to the **independent variable**. This method is often used by **psychologists**.
2) **Field experiments** are a response to the criticisms of lab experiments. They take place outside of the lab in **real social settings** and those involved are often **unaware**. This method is used by **interactionist** sociologists.
3) **Natural experiments** are not set up artificially. An example would be **twin studies**, but these are quite rare.

Twin studies are where you study identical twins (who are genetically identical) in different situations, to see whether something's caused by genetics or if it's caused by socialisation.

**Strengths of lab experiments**

1) The **researcher** has **control** over the experiment.
2) You get **quantitative** data.
3) You can **replicate** the research.

**Limitations of lab experiments**

1) It's **hard** to **reproduce real social situations** in a lab — lab experiments are **artificial**.
2) It's **difficult** to **isolate single variables**. **Social behaviour** is influenced by **many factors**.
3) There are often **moral** and **ethical** issues in lab experiments.
4) People may feel **intimidated** or **act differently** in the lab.

Researchers can measure things in a biased way if they have expectations about the results.

**Strengths of field experiments**

1) They're done in **natural social settings** and are more like **real life**.
2) They can show the **hidden meanings** of **everyday social interaction**.

**Limitations of field experiments**

1) You **can't control the variables** like you can in lab experiments.
2) If people **know they're being studied** they may **change** their **behaviour**.
3) There's an **ethical problem** in carrying out experiments when the subjects **aren't aware** that they are taking part in an experiment.

## *When People Know They're Being Studied, They Sometimes Act Differently*

1) When people are **interested** in something, they **try harder**. They may try harder at what they're doing to get a **positive response** from the researchers. This is called the **Hawthorne Effect**.
2) People try to **figure out** what kind of **response** the **researchers want**. People often either give the researchers the **response they think they want** or the **exact opposite** — depending on whether they want to please the researchers or whether they want to be stubborn.
3) People usually try to show themselves in the **best possible light**. They may say they **wouldn't commit crime** when **really they would**. They may say they **recycle all their rubbish** when **really they don't**.
4) These effects mean data from experiments may **not be valid**.

# Secondary Data

## *Official Statistics are a Source of Secondary Data*

1) **Official statistics** are a source of secondary data. They're produced by local governments, central government and government agencies.
2) **Hard statistics** are **objective**. Politicians can't fiddle with them. Statistics on births and marriages are hard statistics.
3) **Soft statistics** are more **subjective**. Politicians can fiddle with them. Statistics on **crime**, **poverty** and **unemployment** are soft statistics. In the 1980s and 1990s, the government **changed the method** used to **measure unemployment** over 20 times.
4) **Social Trends** is a collection of **regular government surveys** published every year. It's a **great source** of **secondary data**.
5) The **Census** is a survey of every household every 10 years. Every household has to fill in the form **by law**.
6) The **British Crime Survey** looks at victims of crime. The data is collected by a questionnaire.

## *Documents and Mass Media are a Source of Secondary Data*

1) A document is a **written text**. Documents can be **personal** — like **letters**, **diaries**, **autobiographies**, **memoirs** and **suicide notes**. Documents can also be **official**, like **school** records, **health** records, **church** records and **social work** records.
2) Documents can be **expressive** — more to do with **meanings**, like a **suicide note**. Documents can be **formal**, e.g. **official documents. Interpretivists** prefer **expressive** documents because they're a big source of **qualitative data**.
3) **Max Weber** used **historical documents** when he was studying how the **religious** beliefs of Calvinism brought about a **social change**. **Michel Foucault** used **historical documents** to analyse changes in **social control** and **punishment**.
4) There are **problems** with documents. They can be **difficult to understand** if they're old. They might be **fakes**. They might contain **lies** — especially personal documents.
5) The **mass media** is another source of **secondary data** about people and society.
6) Sociologists analyse **documents and the media** by looking at **content**, **themes** and **style of language** used.

## *Sociologists Compare Different Secondary Documents*

1) Sociologists look for **similarities** and **differences** between different secondary documents. They can compare different **times**, different **cultures** and different **groups** within society by looking at secondary data.
2) Researchers can analyse **real social behaviour** and make comparisons without having to set up artificial experiments.
3) Durkheim used this **comparative method** in his famous 1897 study of suicide. He looked at the rates of suicide in different European societies. He found that the suicide rate was **consistent over time**, **but varied between societies** and varied for **different groups** within society.

## *Practice Questions*

Q1 What's meant by an independent variable?

Q2 Name two advantages of field experiments over laboratory experiments.

Q3 What is the Hawthorne effect?

Q4 What is the difference between hard and soft statistics?

**Exam Questions**

Q1 (a) Identify the three main types of experiment that are used in Sociology. (6 marks)

(b) Identify and briefly explain two sources of secondary data. (8 marks)

(c) Evaluate the advantages and disadvantages of experiments to the social scientist. (20 marks)

## *Anyone up for an experiment on how people cope with being millionaires...*

*If you're not really into science, this business about dependent and independent variables might seem a tadge confusing. Don't be too confused — just remember that the dependent variable is the one you measure to see how it's changed. All the stuff on secondary data is fairly straightfoward, I reckon — it's about what kind of secondary data sociologists use.*

# Interpreting Data

*You can interpret, analyse and evaluate data in lots of different ways.*

## Check Data's **Reliable**, **Valid** and **Representative**

**Valid** = data is a **true picture** of **what you're measuring**.
**Reliable** = you can use the **same method again** under the **same conditions** and get the **same results**.
**Representative** = the **sample** has the **same proportions** as the **population**.

## Look for **Correlations** and **Patterns** in **Quantitative** Data

Correlation is where one variable is related to another.

**GCSE attainment by parents' socio-economic classification, 2002**

| | 5 GCSE grades A*-C | 1-4 GCSE grades A*-C | 5 GCSE grades D-G | 1-4 GCSE grades D-G | None reported |
|---|---|---|---|---|---|
| Higher professional | 77 | 13 | 6 | ... | 3 |
| Lower professional | 64 | 21 | 11 | 2 | 2 |
| Intermediate | 52 | 25 | 17 | 2 | 4 |
| Lower supervisory | 35 | 30 | 27 | 4 | 4 |
| Routine | 32 | 32 | 25 | 5 | 6 |
| Other | 32 | 29 | 26 | 4 | 9 |

Published in *Social Trends 34*. Source — Youth Cohort Study.

The appendix of *Social Trends*, tells you that the Youth Cohort study had 35, 000 respondents.

If you were **analysing this data**, you would have to:

1) See **what the table's about**. The **title** tells you that this table is about how **educational achievement** is related to **parents' socio-economic position**.
2) Find out **where it's from**. It says ***Social Trends***. This is a collection of government research. It's possible that there could be political **bias** here.
3) Look for a **correlation** between the variables. In this table, high socio-economic class seems to go with lots of GCSEs at grades A*-C.
4) See what it **tells** you. It says that children with parents in higher socio-economic positions achieve a **higher percentage** of top grades. Children with parents in **lower supervisory** occupations achieve a **higher percentage** of **grades D-G**.
5) Ask if the data is **valid**. The **cause and effect** relationship you can **see** might not be the **only one** there. There's a **correlation**, but it might not be the **cause**. Some sociologists would say that **material deprivation** is the cause but there might be **other causes** that the table just doesn't show.
6) Find out about the **sample**. It's from the **Youth Cohort** study, which has a **large** sample — so you could make **generalisations** about the **population** as a **whole**.
7) Find out about **how** the data was collected. The Youth Cohort study gets its data from school records. You could repeat this study again and get the same results.

If you've got a hypothesis about educational achievement and class, you can use the figures to test it out.

## Question the **Method** and the **Sample** with **Qualitative** Data

"I always leave the quiet ones to just get on with their work. Girls are OK in the class too. It's the boys you have to be tough on. They are usually the trouble makers."

Imagine you got this quote from an **unstructured interview** with a teacher. You would have to:

1) Ask yourself whether the interviewee might have said it because of something to do with the **method**. A **different method** might produce a **different response**, so it might not be very **reliable**.
2) Ask yourself if it's **really what the interviewee believes** or whether they said what they **thought** the **interviewer wanted to hear**. This quote might not be a **true reflection** of how this teacher really acts.
3) See if the sample is **representative**. The research might use a **small** or **untypical sample** — which doesn't tell you much about **teachers in general**.
4) Find out **who carried out the research**. A researcher might have a particular **political** or **sociological point of view**. They can present the research in a way that suits their theories. This is **bias**.
5) Figure out what it **means**. The item tells us something about processes like **labelling** that go on in schools.

# Interpreting Data

## *Analyse **Official Statistics** — They're Not as **Objective** as they First Seem*

Official statistics are a **really useful** source of **existing information**. Some sociologists love them because they're **cheap** and **available** (fnar, fnar...). With **official statistics**, you can look at **trends** over **time**. The sample sizes tend to be **huge**, so at least you know they're **representative**. Official stats are sometimes your **only source of information**. There are some **problems** with them, though — they don't always **measure** what they **say** they measure.

1) **Positivists** like official stats — they think official stats are a source of **objective**, **reliable** data. They **analyse** the relationship between **social variables** and look for **correlations** and **cause and effect relationships**.
2) **Marxists** say that **official statistics** are **Government statistics**. They think all official stats are **politically biased** to serve the **interests of the ruling class**, and **designed** to **avoid political embarrassment**.
3) **Interactionists** say that **official statistics** are **not hard facts**. They are **not as objective** as they **first seem**. They reckon **statistics** are **social constructions** and don't tell you about **meanings** and **motives**.

**Example — crime statistics** don't tell you an **objective figure** of how many **crimes** are committed.
The police **don't know about all crimes** that are committed. Some criminals get **let off**. Some people **don't trust the police** enough to **tell** them about a crime. Some people might not **realise** they're a victim of crime. So — there's crime that we **plain don't know about** if we rely on **official statistics**.

## *Analyse **Content** of **Documents** and the **Mass Media** — but **Take Care**...*

1) Traditional **quantitative content analysis** produces **statistical data**.
2) For example, you can **count** the **number of times something happens** in a **TV programme** — like the number of times girls are in a passive role.
3) The research is **reliable**, **easy to obtain** and you can **make comparisons**.
4) The problem is that the **researchers' interpretations** may be **biased**. Researchers **might not agree** on exactly what counts as a "passive role" for example.
5) You still have a lot of **explaining** to do even if you have a **clear result** like "ethnic minorities are under-represented in TV programmes". You have to explain **how** and **why**.

**Qualitative content analysis** looks for **themes** and **meanings** in media and documents. **Interactionists** prefer this method because it **uncovers hidden meanings**. It's more **valid** than quantitative analysis. The down side is that the researcher can **interpret** the sources in **different ways**. It's not very **reliable**.

**John Scott (1990)** thinks sociologists should be **really careful** when **analysing secondary sources**.

1) Documents might **not** be **authentic** — they might be **fakes**.
2) They might **not** be **credible** — the author might not be telling the **truth**.
3) They might **not** be **representative**.
4) They might be **difficult to understand** — words might have had different **meanings** in the past than they do now.

## *Practice Questions*

Q1 How are the methods used to analyse quantitative data different to those used for qualitative data?

Q2 Name a strength of official statistics.

Q3 How would interactionists criticise official statistics?

Q4 What does John Scott (1990) say about analysing documents?

**Exam Questions**

Q1 (a) What is meant by the term reliability? (2 marks)
(b) Suggest three problems sociologists can have when analysing documents. (6 marks)
(c) Examine the advantages and disadvantages of official statistics as a source of data for the sociologist. (20 marks)

## *I'm looking for patterns in an Argyle jumper...*

*In the exam, you might be given a set of data to make sense of. Make sure you go through it like these pages tell you to, and you'll be fine. Always look at how data's collected, the sample size, bias, validity and reliability. Don't get validity and reliability confused, will you. People seem to get them mixed up in the exam, and it'll lose you marks.*

# Limitations of Research

*Research has its limits — it can't tell you everything. Here are the pros and cons of different kinds of data.*

## Primary Data is Collected First Hand — it has Good Points and Bad Points

Researchers collect primary information themselves. You could use methods like **interviews**, **questionnaires**, **observations**, **ethnography** or **experiments**. You can gather quantitative or qualitative data.

1) Primary data is **first hand research**. It doesn't rely on **another sociologist's research** and you can carefully **choose your method** to make your data as valid and reliable as possible.
2) Primary data is always **brand new** and **bang up to date**.
3) **Some methods** of getting primary data can be **expensive** and **time-consuming**.
4) **Some methods** may put the researcher in a **dangerous situation**.
5) **Some methods** may be **unethical** if you don't get **informed consent**.
6) The **researcher's own values** may mess with the research process. This creates **bias**.
7) You **can't always get access** to the group you want to study.

## Secondary Data is Existing Information — it has Pros and Cons

Secondary data includes **official statistics**, **diaries**, **letters**, **memoirs**, **emails**, **TV documentaries** and **newspapers** as sources. You gather the data together and analyse it, but you don't generate the data.

1) You can **quickly** and easily collect secondary data.
2) You can **easily** use **secondary data** to **compare different societies**.
3) With secondary data you can study **past events and societies**. You can **compare past** and **present**.
4) You don't have to worry about **informed consent**.
5) The **existing data** may not be **valid** or **reliable** — you're **stuck** with the way the research was **originally done**.
6) Documents may not be **authentic**, **representative** or **credible**. Official statistics can be **biased**.
7) You **might not be able to find** the information that you need from existing data.
8) **Your values** don't influence the **collection** of the data, but the **researcher's values** might have ruined the validity of the **original research**. **Your values** can get in the way of **how you analyse** the data.

## Quantitative Data Can be Reliable but Not Very Valid

1) With quantitative data, you can **test your hypothesis** and look for **cause and effect** relationships.
2) You can **compare** your statistics against existing statistics, and look for **trends over time** and **between societies**.
3) It's **easy** to **analyse tables**, **charts** and **graphs** — especially line charts, bar graphs and pie charts.
4) You can **repeat** questionnaires and structured interviews to **test reliability**.
5) Quantitative methods allow **large samples** so the findings **represent** the **general population**.
6) **Statistics** can **hide reality**. **Categories** in **interviews** or **questionnaires** can **distort** the truth.
7) They don't tell you anything about the **meanings** and **motives** and **reasons** behind behaviour — there's not much **depth** or **insight** into **social interaction**.
8) They can be **politically biased**. The method may have been chosen in order to get the "right" data.

## Qualitative Data can be Valid but Not Very Reliable

1) **Qualitative data** gives **insight** into **social interaction**. It's a **detailed description** of social behaviour.
2) Qualitative data lets you find out the **meanings** and **motives** behind behaviour.
3) You don't have to **force** people into **artificial categories** like in questionnaires.
4) Qualitative methods let you build up **trust** and research **sensitive topics**.
5) Qualitative methods are **difficult to repeat** — they **aren't very reliable**.
6) The research is often on a **small scale** — so the findings might not **represent** the whole population.
7) **Positivists** say qualitative results **lack credibility** because they're **subjective** and open to interpretation.
8) The **researcher** can get the **wrong end of the stick** and **misinterpret** the group or individual they're studying.

# Limitations of Research

## *Triangulation is When You Combine Methods or Data*

Triangulation is when sociologists try to combine different methods or data to **get the best out of all of them**.

1) **Triangulation** gives a more **detailed picture** than when you only use **one method**, so it's more **valid**.
2) When you triangulate, you can **check different sets of data against each other**, so it's more **reliable**.
3) Triangulation combines the **strengths** and the **weaknesses** of different types of data.
4) It can be **expensive** and **time-consuming** to do the same research with lots of methods.
5) Sometimes, it's **not possible** to use triangulation — you might only be able to use **one method**, or there might not be very many **different kinds of data** for what you're studying.

### Eileen Barker (1984) studied the Moonies

The Moonies are a religious organisation, also known as the Unification Church. Barker used **in-depth interviews**, **overt participant observation** and **questionnaires**. She used questionnaires to test out hypotheses that she'd thought of after doing the interviews and observations.

### Mac an Ghaill (1994) studied masculinity

He used **overt participant observation** and **interviews** with young straight men and young gay men. He **discussed ideas** about what made a man masculine. He didn't just observe the young men and try to figure out what they thought.

## *Research Results can be Reported in Books and Journals*

Sociological research is published in **books** or in **journals** like the *British Journal of Sociology* (BJS). Journals give very specific **guidelines** on how to write the report. The BJS has **rules** about spelling, grammar, length and **avoiding sexist** and **racist language**. There are also **ethical** guidelines to follow.

All journal articles tend to follow a **similar pattern**:

1) **Abstract** — a **small paragraph** which **briefly** describes **intentions**, **results** and **conclusion**.
2) **Introduction** — explains what's being investigated and why.
3) **Methods** — describes the **methods** used and **why they were chosen**.
4) **Results** — presented with tables, charts, quotes etc.
5) **Discussion** — the **significance** of the results, any **methodological problems**, any **suggestions** of **new social policy**.
6) **References** — a list of the books, journals, websites and newspapers that were used.

**Quantitative data** is reported in the form of **tables**, **figures**, **pie charts**, **line graphs** and **bar charts**.
**Qualitative data** is reported in the form of **quotes**. If you were researching bullying with **unstructured interviews** you might **quote** different people's **feelings** about being bullied. You can stick the whole **interview transcripts** at the end in the **appendix**.

## *Practice Questions*

Q1 Give three disadvantages of primary data.
Q2 Name a strength of quantitative data.
Q3 What is secondary data?
Q4 Name a limitation of secondary data.
Q5 What is triangulation?
Q6 What pattern do journal articles usually follow?

**Exam Question**

Q1 Compare the strengths and weaknesses of qualitative and quantitative forms of data. (20 marks)

## *Oops, my revision's just done some Bermuda triangulation...*

*When you discuss a method in the Exam try to include some examples of studies which used it. This shows the Examiner that you understand what kind of research the method works best for. It'll also give you a chance to show off your wider sociological knowledge which always goes down well with the Examiners — it might even get you a few extra marks.*

# Do Well in Your Exam

*These two pages are all about how to do well in your exams.*

## Units 1 and 2 each have 3 Core Areas

1) **Units 1 and 2** each have **three core areas**. Unit 1 has 'Families and Households', 'Health', and 'Mass Media'. Unit 2 has 'Education', 'Wealth, Poverty and Welfare' and 'Work and Leisure'. You will have been taught at least **one core area for each unit**.
2) The exam papers for units 1 and 2 are worth **60 marks** each and are each **1 hour 15 minutes** long.
3) In the exam, there's **one long question** about **each core area** in the unit. You only have to do **one** of these long questions. Make sure you **choose** the **unit** which you have been **taught and revised**.
4) Each long question has **six parts** to it — (a) to (f). There's always a **source** or two to read at the start.
   - **Part (a)** is worth **2 marks,** and asks you to define a term or phrase from the sources.
   - **Parts (b)-(d)** are worth **4, 6** and **8 marks** respectively — they ask you to give **examples** of something, give **reasons** for something, or **briefly explain something**.
   - **Parts (e)** and **(f)** are **essay questions**, worth **20 marks each**. In part **(f)**, you have to **refer to one of the sources**.

## Unit 3 is about Sociological Methods

1) **Unit 3** is 'Sociological Methods'. This exam is worth **60 marks** too but you only get an **hour** to do it.
2) There's **one big question** which you have to answer — you don't get any choice on this paper.
3) The question has a similar layout to units 1 and 2:
   - You get **two sources** to read, which can be **descriptions** of a **sociological study** or **articles** about **sociological methods**.
   - You get asked **four simple questions** worth between **2 marks** and **10 marks** — you have to define something or write about the problems with a particular method.
   - Then you get two long essay questions worth **20 marks** each. In one of them, you **have to refer** to **one of the sources** you've been given.

## You Get Marks For...

AO just means 'Assessment Objective'

### You Get Marks for **AO1 — Knowledge and Understanding** and **AO2 — Identification, Analysis, Interpretation and Evaluation**

**Part (a)-(d) questions** mainly ask you to demonstrate your **knowledge and understanding (AO1)** of the theories, studies and concepts of the module that you've studied. You'll be asked to explain terms, identify reasons and explain key ideas. You might also be asked to identify criticisms of a theory or idea.

**Part (e) and (f) questions** test **AO1 skills** *and* **AO2 skills**. Part **(e)** has **14 marks** for AO1 and **6 marks** for AO2. Part **(f)** has **6 marks** for AO1 and **14 marks** for AO2. So it's **most important** to **demonstrate your AO2 skills in part (f)**.

For AO2 marks you need to do things like:

1) **Choose relevant information / studies** for answering the question.
2) Present the **strengths and weaknesses** of a theory / study.
3) Present **alternative** explanations / interpretations of findings.
4) Use the material to provide a **commentary** — a well-argued essay.

Oh... and don't forget **the basics**.

The AQA examiners really care about stuff like being able to read your handwriting — they're always going on about it in their examiners' reports.

- Write as **neatly** as you can.
- Use good **grammar** and **punctuation**.
- Check your **spelling** — especially of words to do with Sociology.
- Make sure you **answer the question**.

## Here are some Hints for Short Answer Questions

1) If you're asked for **two** things, give **two** things. **Not one**. Not three. Or four. Five is right out.
2) If you're asked for two things, spend **equal time and effort** on **both**. You **won't** get as many marks for a **lopsided** answer.
3) Give **examples** from **sociological studies** and from **statistics** to **back up** your points.
4) Refer to **sociological theories** like Marxism, Functionalism, Interactionism — but **only** if they're **relevant**.
5) Use the **number of marks** as a **guide** for **how long you should spend on each question**. The more marks a question is worth, the longer you should spend answering it.

# References

***These are details of studies which are discussed in the Revision Guide.***


Skeggs, B. (1991) 'Challenging masculinity and using sexuality' (*British Journal of Sociology of Education*, vol.12, no.2)

Smith, J. (1987) *Different for Girls: How Culture Creates Women* (London: Chatto and Windus)

Solomos, J. (1993) *Race and Racism in Britain* (London: Macmillan)

Spender, D. (1983) *Invisible Women: Schooling and Scandal* (London: Women's Press)

Stacey, J. (1990) *Brave New Families: Stories of Domestic Upheaval in Late Twentieth Century America* (New York: Basic Books)

Stanworth, M. (1983) *Gender and Schooling: A Study of Sexual Divisions in the Classroom* (London: Hutchinson)

Sugarman, B. (1970) 'Social Class, Values and Behaviour in Schools' in Craft, M. (ed.) *Family, Class and Education* (London: Longman)

Swann Report (1985) *Education for All* (London: HMSO)

Szasz, T. (1971) *The Manufacture of Madness* (London: Routledge & Kegan Paul)

Thompson, E.P. (1967) 'Time, Work Discipline and Industrial Capitalism' (*Past and Present* no. 38)

Thompson, P. (1989) 'The End of Bureaucracy' in Haralambos, M. (ed.) *The Labour Process: Changing Theory and Changing Practice* (London)

Townsend, P. (1970) *The Concept of Poverty* (London: Heinemann)

Townsend, P. (1979) *Poverty in the United Kingdom* (Harmondsworth: Penguin)

Tuchman (1978) *Hearth and Home: Images of Women in the Mass Media* (New York: Oxford University Press)

Tudor Hart, J. (1971) 'The Inverse Care Law' (*The Lancet* Saturday 27th Feb.)

Tumin, M. M. (1967) 'Some Principles of Stratification: A Critical Analysis' in Bendix and Lipset (eds.) *Social Stratification: The Forms and Functions of Social Inequality* (Englewood Cliffs, NJ: Prentice Hall)

Turkle (1996) *Life on the Screen: Identity in the Age of the Internet.* (London: Weidenfeld and Nicholson)

Van Dijk (1991) *Racism and the Press* (London: Routledge & Kegan Paul)

Walker, A. (1990) 'Blaming the Victims' in Murray, C. *The Emerging British Underclass* (London: IEA)

Walker, C. and Walker, A. (1994) 'Poverty and the Poor' in Haralambos (ed.) *Developments in Sociology Vol. 10*

Weber, M. (1958) *The Protestant Work Ethic and the Spirit of Capitalism* (New York: Scribner's Sons)

Wedderburn, D. (1974) *Poverty, Inequality and Class Structure* (Cambridge: CUP)

Westergaard, J. and Resler, H. (1976) *Class in a Capitalist Society* (Harmondsworth: Penguin)

Willis, P. (1977) *Learning to Labour: How Working Class Kids Get Working Class Jobs* (London: Saxon House)

Wilmott, P. (1988) 'Urban Kinship Past and Present' (*Social Studies Review*, Nov.)

Wilmott and Young (1960) *Family and Class in a London Suburb* (London: Routledge & Kegan Paul)

Wilmott and Young (1973) *The Symmetrical Family* (Harmondsworth: Penguin)

Woods, P. (1983) *Sociology and the School: An Interactionist Viewpoint* (London: Routledge & Kegan Paul)

Woolf, N. (1990) *The Beauty Myth* (Chatto and Windus)

Wright, C. (1992) 'Early Education: Multiracial Primary School Classrooms' in Gill, Mayor and Blair (eds.) *Racism and Education* (London: Sage)

Wright Mills, C. (1951) *White Collar: The American Middle Classes* (New York: Oxford University Press)

Zaretsky, E. (1976) *Capitalism, The Family and Professional Life* (London: Pluto Press)

Zimbalist, A. (1979) *Case Studies on the Labour Process* (London: Monthly Review Press)

Zuboff, S. (1988) *In the Age of the Smart Machine* (New York: Basic Books)


*Every effort has been made to ensure these references are as accurate and comprehensive as possible. For those studies where it has been difficult to obtain full details, we would be grateful for information. Please contact the publisher if you notice any inaccuracies or omissions, and we will gladly update the book at the next reprint. Thank you.*

# Glossary

**absolute poverty** Not having the essentials needed for life — food, warmth and shelter.

**achieved status** Status you get by working for it.

**affluent workers** Workers who do boring jobs that pay well so they can have a nice life outside work.

**alienated labour** Work that's turned into a lot of boring meaningless tasks, where workers have no say in what they do, and not enough share of the profits.

**allocation function** Sorting people out into appropriate jobs depending on their skills.

**anomie** A state of confusion where the norms of society break down.

**ascribed status** Status you have from birth.

**Bourdieu, Pierre** French sociologist who came up with the idea of cultural capital.

**bourgeoisie** Marx's term for the capitalist class.

**capitalism** In basic terms, this means employers buy workers' labour in return for wages, and sell the things the workers make for profit. A capitalist economic system allows individuals to use their assets and initiative to create profit in competitive business conditions.

**censorship** Controlling what can and can't be printed and broadcast.

**class** Division of society based on how people earn money.

**collective consciousness** The shared values and norms that hold society together.

**communism** A system of government which is theoretically based on a classless society and where private ownership has been abolished.

**conform** To go along with society's norms and values.

**conjugal roles** Husband and wife roles — who does the paid work, who does the washing up etc.

**consensus** A shared agreement.

**cultural capital** The cultural skills and know-how that children learn from their parents.

**cultural deprivation theory** A theory that says working class culture makes people disadvantaged.

**culture** A way of life, a set of norms and values.

**deferred gratification** Working towards the promise of future reward. Associated with middle-class values.

**delinquency** Bad behaviour and social disruption. Includes criminal behaviour and plain annoying behaviour.

**deskilled labour** Where a job used to need skill, but doesn't any more.

**deviant** Something that goes against society's norms and values. Deviant behaviour is behaviour that society doesn't approve of.

**discourse** Any kind of discussion or talk about something.

**Durkheim, Emile (1858-1917)** French founding father of sociology. He thought that different parts of society had different roles, like the organs of the body.

**ethnic group** A group of people with a common cultural and racial background — sharing the same language, religion and way of life.

**ethnocentric** Centred around the values and interests of one particular ethnic group.

**ethnography** Studying the way of life of people by observation, interviews, case studies etc.

**extended family** A social unit comprising the nuclear family *and* other relatives, e.g. uncles, aunts, grandparents. Often includes three or more generations of the same family.

**false consciousness** Marxism says that workers are in a state of false consciousness about their place in society. Workers don't realise how unfair it is. If they did, they'd start a revolution.

**false needs** Herbert Marcuse said that workers are fed the idea that they "need" fancy goods that they don't really need at all.

**feminism** Belief that women are disadvantaged in society, and that women and men should have equal rights. Feminist sociologists think that mainstream sociology has ignored the lives of women.

**folk devil** A scapegoat for things going wrong in society.

**Functionalism** The belief that everything in society exists for a reason.

**gender** Masculinity and femininity. Sociologists say that gender is a social construction. Being male or female is the biological sex you're born with, while masculinity and femininity are identities you're socialised into.

**globalisation** The breaking down of traditional national boundaries. This happens due to factors such as the growth of multinational companies, increased migration of people between societies, and the global marketing of culture products.

**Hall, Stuart (b. 1932)** British sociologist, big on studying ethnicity and popular culture.

**hegemony** The domination of one group of people over another, or of one set of ideas over another.

**hidden curriculum** The social norms and values that are taught at school, but not as part of the regular curriculum. Includes conformity, respect for authority and other cultural values.

**hierarchy** A system which ranks people according to status. Any system where you have a boss in charge of people is a hierarchy.

**household** A group of people who live together. They needn't be related.

**hypothetico-deductive model** Where you come up with an idea (a hypothesis) and do experiments to test if it's true or not.

**iatrogenesis** Health problems caused by the medical system.

**identity** An individual's concept of themselves. This can be related to class, gender, ethnicity.

**ideology** A set of ideas and beliefs.

**industrial action** Action that workers take in disputes with their bosses — includes strike, sabotage, work to rule, absenteeism.

**industrialisation** The large-scale development of industry.

**infrastructure** The economic structure of society.

**institutional racism** When the policies, attitudes and actions of an institution discriminate against ethnic minorities — sometimes unintentionally.

**institutions of society** Things like the family, religion, the education system, the healthcare system.

**Interactionism** A sociological approach which focuses on the actions and the thoughts of individuals. Also called **interpretivism**.

**internalised norms and values** Norms and values that have become part of who you are and the way you think.

# Glossary

**interpretivism** See interactionism.

**labelling theory** This theory says that labelling someone as deviant will make them more deviant.

**left-wing** A general term for the political "left" — including socialism and Marxism. Left-wing thinkers and politicians usually support reform to achieve greater economic and social equality. Many different views can be called "left-wing" — including both moderate and extreme standpoints.

**longitudinal study** A study done over a period of time.

**Marcuse, Herbert (1898-1979)** German Neo-Marxist sociologist who had the idea of false needs.

**Marx, Karl (1818-1883)** German social theorist who wrote *Das Capital* and came up with the somewhat influential theory about power being the control of the means of production.

**Marxism** The belief that society is divided into the bourgeoisie, who own the "means of production", and the proletariat, who do the work. The bourgeoisie or capitalist class exploit the workers, and arrange society to keep the workers down. Most of the profit from the work that the proletariat do is kept by the bourgeoisie.

**mass media** Newspapers, TV, magazines, radio, Internet — media that lots of people use and consume.

**master status** A label has master status when it's the most important thing about you and it rules how other people view you and how you behave.

**meritocracy** A system where the best (most talented and hard-working) people rise to the top.

**moral panic** A fear of a moral crisis in society. Moral panics are usually linked to "folk devils". The mass media have a big role in stirring up moral panics in modern society.

**Murray, Charles** American New Right sociologist who believes that there's an underclass who are too dependent on benefits.

**nonconformity** Not going along with society's norms and values.

**norm** A behaviour that's considered normal in a particular society, e.g. queuing, wearing clothes, making some eye contact when talking to someone.

**nuclear family** Mum, dad and children living together.

**Oakley, Ann** Feminist sociologist who studied housework and gender socialisation.

**Parsons, Talcott (1902-1979)** American Functionalist sociologist who wrote about the structure and functions of society.

**patriarchy** A society where men are dominant. Feminists often describe male-dominated societies and institutions as "patriarchal."

**peer groups** Groups of people who all have the same status in society.

**pluralism** The belief that society is made of lots of different parts, and that each of those parts gets their say, via democracy and a free market.

**positivism** A theoretical point of view which concentrates on social facts, scientific method and quantitative data (facts and figures).

**post-Fordism** A new type of flexible work and management.

**postmodernism** A movement that emphasises a mix-and-match approach to values, and which says there isn't a single objective truth.

**postmodernity** The world after the modern age — with flexible working, individual responsibility and people constructing their own identity.

**qualitative methods of research** Methods like unstructured interviews and participant observation that give results which tell a story about individuals' lives.

**quantitative methods of research** Methods like surveys and structured interviews that give results which you can easily put into a graph or table.

**reliability** Data is reliable if you can do the same research again and get the same results.

**right-wing** A general term for the political "right" — including both moderate and extreme standpoints. Right-wing thinkers and politicians tend to be conservative — supporting traditional values and sometimes resisting change. Right-wing politics are often associated with capitalist economic values.

**self-fulfilling prophecy** When people behave in the way that they know others have predicted.

**social construct** An idea or belief that's created in society, and doesn't come from a scientific fact.

**social democrats** People who think the state should redistribute wealth, and that there should be a strong welfare state paid for out of taxes.

**social policy** Things that governments do that affect society, e.g. raising taxes, having a free healthcare system, allowing schools to run their own budgets, changing divorce laws.

**stereotype** A generalisation about a social group — often inaccurate and insulting.

**stratification** The way society is divided up into layers or classes.

**stratified sample** A sample with the same proportions of gender or class or age as the population you're studying.

**subculture** A group who share values and norms which are different from mainstream ones.

**superstructure** The cultural structure of society.

**symmetrical family** A family structure where conjugal (husband and wife) roles are shared.

**text** Any piece of media — a book, a TV programme, an advert, a photo.

**third way politics** A political viewpoint that combines elements of right wing self-sufficiency and left wing social democracy.

**triangulation** Combining different methods and data to get results which are both valid and reliable.

**universal benefit** Benefit that everyone gets, whether they're rich or poor.

**urbanisation** The expansion of cities and towns. Often linked to industrialisation, with rural workers moving to urban areas to get jobs in industry.

**validity** Data is valid if it gives an accurate picture.

**values** Beliefs or standards shared in a society.

**vocational education** Learning skills specific to the needs of the workplace.

**Weber, Max (1864-1920)** German academic, considered to be the father of modern sociology.

**Willis, Paul (b. 1945)** Sociologist who studied working class boys and their anti-school subcultures.

# Index

# Index

# Index